SEGREGATED
SCHOOLS

Positions: Education, Politics, and Culture
Edited by Kenneth J. Saltman, DePaul University,
and Ron Scapp, College of Mount St. Vincent

Affirmative Action:
Racial Preference in Black and White
Tim J. Wise

The Edison Schools:
Corporate Schooling and the Assault on Public Education
Kenneth J. Saltman

School Commercialism:
From Democratic Ideal to Market Commodity
Alex Molnar

Segregated Schools:
Educational Apartheid in Post-Civil Rights America
Paul Street

SEGREGATED SCHOOLS

EDUCATIONAL
APARTHEID
IN
POST-CIVIL
RIGHTS
AMERICA

PAUL STREET

Routledge
Taylor & Francis Group
New York London

Published in 2005 by
Routledge
Taylor & Francis Group
270 Madison Avenue
New York, NY 10016

Published in Great Britain by
Routledge
Taylor & Francis Group
2 Park Square
Milton Park, Abingdon
Oxon OX14 4RN

© 2005 by Taylor & Francis Group, LLC
Routledge is an imprint of Taylor & Francis Group

Printed in the United States of America on acid-free paper
10 9 8 7 6 5 4 3 2 1

International Standard Book Number-10: 0-415-95115-1 (Hardcover) 0-415-95116-X (Softcover)
International Standard Book Number-13: 978-0-415-95115-9 (Hardcover) 978-0-415-95116-6 (Softcover)
Library of Congress Card Number 2005005276

Library of Congress Cataloging-in-Publication Data

Street, Paul Louis.
    Segregated schools : educational apartheid in post-civil rights America / Paul Street.
        p. cm. -- (Positions : education, politics, and culture)
    Includes bibliographical references and index.
    ISBN 0-415-95115-1 (hb : alk. paper) -- ISBN 0-415-95116-X (pb : alk. paper)
    1. Segregation in education--United States. 2. Educational equalization--United States.
I. Title. II. Series: Positions (Routledge(Firm))

LC212.52.S87 2005
379.2'63'0973--dc22   2005005276

Taylor & Francis Group
is the Academic Division of T&F Informa plc.

Visit the Taylor & Francis Web site at
http://www.taylorandfrancis.com

and the Routledge Web site at
http://www.routledge-ny.com

Let us be dissatisfied until America will no longer have a high blood pressure of creeds and an anemia of deeds. Let us be dissatisfied until the tragic walls that separate the outer city of wealth and comfort and the inner city of poverty and despair shall be crushed by the battering ram of the forces of justice. Let us be dissatisfied until those who live on the outskirts of hope are brought into the metropolis of daily security. Let us be dissatisfied until slums are cast into the junk heaps of history, and every family is living in a decent sanitary home. Let us be dissatisfied until the dark yesterdays of segregated schools will be transformed into bright tomorrows of quality, integrated education. Let us be dissatisfied until integration is not seen as a problem but as an opportunity to participate in the beauty of diversity.

—Martin Luther King, Jr.,
"Where Do We Go From Here?" (1967)

Contents

SERIES EDITORS' INTRODUCTION

"Positions" is a series interrogating the intersections of education, politics, and culture. Books in the series are short, polemical, and accessibly written, merging rigorous scholarship with politically engaged criticism. They focus on both pressing contemporary topics and historical issues that continue to define and inform the relationship between education and society.

Positions as a term refers to the obvious position that authors in the series take, but it might also refer to the "war of position" described by Italian cultural theorist Antonio Gramsci, who emphasized the centrality of political struggles over meanings, language, and ideas, to the battle for civil society. We believe that these struggles over meanings, language, and ideas are crucial for the making of a more just social order in which political, cultural, and economic power is democratically controlled. We believe, as Paulo Freire emphasized, that there is no way not to take a position.

Paul Street's book in the series, *Segregated Schools*, takes a position against racial segregation, not only in schools but in the plethora of institutions and practices where it is presently found. On first glance an argument against racial segregation would seem to be too obvious an argument to make. After all, few Americans would openly admit their desire for segregation. And yet American apartheid persists with such a vengeance that the dream of integration has fallen out of common-sense talk and imagination. Paul Street explains why. His book is not only rich in information and deeply historical; it also situates the history of racial segregation in schooling within broader political and economic domestic and international contexts. This volume provides indispensable tools for the crucial project to dismantle segregation in schools and throughout society as necessary conditions for the development of a genuine democracy.

KENNETH J. SALTMAN
ASSISTANT PROFESSOR, SOCIAL AND CULTURAL STUDIES IN EDUCATION
DEPAUL UNIVERSITY

RON SCAPP
ASSOCIATE PROFESSOR OF EDUCATION AND PHILOSOPHY
DIRECTOR OF THE MASTER'S PROGRAM IN URBAN AND
MULTICULTURAL EDUCATION
THE COLLEGE OF MOUNT SAINT VINCENT

INTRODUCTION

No Birthday Bash for *Brown*

Fifty-one years ago, on May 17, 1954, the United States Supreme
Court ruled, in the landmark *Brown v. Board of Education* decision, that legal race separation was inherently unequal and
therefore unconstitutional in public education. Last year, that
historic court case was remembered and assessed in hundreds
of special commemorative events. I was involved in the organization of one such event—a day-long conference that brought
together a number of leading scholars and policymakers to
evaluate the lessons and legacy of the ruling and the subsequent struggle for black educational integration and equality.
At this gathering, and at numerous other similar proceed-
ings, the feeling was remarkably somber. The speakers, most
especially black speakers, were in no mood to throw *Brown* a

celebratory half-century birthday bash. The spirit of *Brown's* fifty-year commemoration was notably bittersweet.

There were a number of sound reasons for this refusal to mark *Brown's* anniversary in festive terms. The decision itself was anything but a forthright assault on racial segregation and inequality. Consistent with its tepid language, which avoided direct confrontation with the core white-supremacist ideologies and structures of the long segregationist "Jim Crow" era, *Brown* failed to mandate a reasonably rapid remedy for the crime of legal educational apartheid. It was left to activists, a great subsequent civil rights movement (itself sparked in no small part by *Brown*), and succeeding rulings and legislation to put substantive policy meat on the legal bones of *Brown* and to extend the logic of desegregation beyond public schooling.

Above all, the sober tone of *Brown's* official remembrance reflected harsh contemporary realities. As the leading black American journalist Ellis Cose noted in a coldly accurate assessment in *Newsweek's* May 17, 2004 edition, the *Brown* decision "rested on an assumption that simply wasn't true: that once formal, state-mandated segregation ended, 'equal educational opportunities' would be the result. A half century later, school segregation is far from dead and the goal of educational equality is as elusive as ever."[1]

There were, to be sure, real school-integrationist victories, especially in the South and during the second decade out from *Brown.* Fifty-one years later, after countless desegregation battles within and beyond courtrooms, American schools are not nearly as racially separated as they were in 1954, when official segregation existed in seventeen states and the nation's capital; four in ten U.S. students attended schools that were racially separated by law. Prior to *Brown* nearly every black student south of the Mason-Dixon line was enrolled in a 100 percent nonwhite school. Currently, the vast majority of black students attend integrated schools, thanks in no small measure to *Brown* and the civil rights revolution it helped inspire.

Nonetheless, the racial composition of the nation's school districts mirrors its starkly segregated residential landscape, reflecting and furthering the division of our great metropolitan areas between disproportionately black, Latino and poor cities and more affluent, predominantly white suburbs. And "while the principle of affirmative action under the trendy code word 'diversity' has brought unparalleled integration into higher education, the military, and corporate America,"[2] the United States has been moving backward over the last twenty-five years to a system of deeply entrenched educational apartheid that both feeds and reflects broader patterns of racial and class inequity. During the last three decades, much of the flesh of desegregation has been stripped from *Brown*'s legal skeleton. Public school integration has been disassembled on the interconnected killing and cutting floors of judicial regression, housing segregation, and "white flight."

Significantly reduced partly because of school desegregation during the 1960s and 1970s, the much-bemoaned black-white student "achievement gap" has widened since the 1970s. This has grave implications for the life chances of black youth in a time when the higher education income premium—the earnings gap between those with and those without college degrees—is at an all-time high and few decent jobs remain for people with only a high school degree or less. Students in many of the nation's deeply shamed inner-city schools know more about the names of their state's prisons than they do about those of their state's universities.

Brown's promise of educational equality for children of color remains as unfulfilled as is its pledge of integration. As before *Brown*, racial school separation in the United States translates into racial school inequality within a broader context of persistent white structural and ideological supremacy. An unrelenting strong connection between minority status and poverty in the United States is reflected and exacerbated by a privilege-preserving minority school funding gap that results largely from the nation's tendency to rely heavily on local property wealth to pay for public schools. Inner-city black and Latino students suffer disproportionately from rotting school structures, inadequate school materials, chronic instability and under-qualification on the part of their teachers, and overcrowded classrooms with inordinately high student-teacher ratios. Students' struggle for quality education is too often undermined by teachers, school officials, and a broader culture that see those students as incapable of grasping elevated concepts, moving into higher education, finding good jobs, and functioning as full citizens. Inner-city students of color are especially targeted by the authoritarian and mind- and soul-deadening standardized-test-based curriculum that public authorities inflict with particular intensity on urban minorities and poor.

Things are very different in shiny white suburban schools that serve as de facto private college preparatory academies within the "public" system. These schools attract many of the best, most energized teachers who are eager for the opportunity to practice their craft in safe and pleasing structures with low student-teacher ratios. They enjoy the best and latest materials and the freedom to challenge students who expect to spend their late teens and early twenties in higher education and not, as is common for black male youth, under the supervision of the criminal justice system. Even within technically integrated and well-funded schools and school districts, moreover, black and Latino students continue to undergo significantly separate and unequal school experiences.

But the deepest inequalities originate and operate outside of the schools, largely beyond the reach of schools and educational policy. They are found in the total environment of the urban ghettoes where nearly half the nation's black children live. The nation's many predominantly black and Hispanic schools are packed with children who bring enormous, heavily racialized social-class barriers to learning that few white children must overcome. No matter how "good" or "bad" their schools, these students deal with an imposing, interconnected array of stunning educational obstacles resulting from poverty as well as a large number of related "extra-school" factors. They come from communities marked by low income, massive unemployment, political isolation, high crime, rampant incarceration and widespread possession of felony records, poor physical and mental health, widespread violence, extreme stress, environmental pollution, and stark family fragility.

In some ways, racial segregation and inequity in American schools seem more deeply entrenched today than at the time of *Brown*. To understand this irony, the first chapter of this book will argue, it is necessary to distinguish between overt public and legal racism and covert societal and institutional racism. The first type of racism is largely defeated in the United States, but the second and deeper level of racism is alive and well. It involves the operation of supposedly racially neutral or "color-blind" social forces, policies, and practices—including America's uniquely heavy reliance on local property taxes to fund public schools and on "high-stakes testing" to measure, reward, and punish school and student performance—that "just happen" to disproportionately and negatively affect people of color. More than simply outliving the explicit, open and public racism of the past, it is partly strengthened by past civil rights victories—including formal legal school desegregation. Those triumphs encourage the illusion of racism's disappearance and the notions that the only barriers left to black equality in the United States are internal to the black community and that disadvantaged African Americans are personally responsible for their presence at the bottom of the U.S. hierarchy. Overt racism is easier to identify and to resist than the covert "color-blind" and "new age" racism that sorts black and Latino children into persistently separate and unequal schools and communities fifty years after *Brown*.[3]

To make matters yet worse, twenty-first century U.S. educational race apartheid is deepened by the ascendancy of neoliberal policy and ideology, which attack core moral and political bases for meaningful public commitment to equal minority education and intensify the steep disadvantages that many nonwhite children bring to the classroom. As the prolific educational theorist Henry A. Giroux has argued, neoliberalism's terrible consequences for children and public schools are compounded by the related ascendancy of a "belligerent [neoconservative] nationalism" that "constructs community on the basis of fear" and "mindless conformity" rather than "democratic possibility." Increasingly shorn of social-democratic "helping functions" and reduced to its expanding "policing" role in relation to the poor and minorities, the American public sector in the neoliberal era is being transformed into a regressive and oppressive "garrison state"—one that values prisons and empire over quality public education and welfare. It increasingly acts as little more than the "authoritarian agent of capital's dictates," replacing compassion with repression and "criminalizing social problems" that result from the worsening socioeconomic and related racial inequalities that are generated and exacerbated by its own plutocratic and repressive policies and practices.[4] This reactionary and authoritarian devolution falls most terribly on communities of color.

The chasm between color-blind promise and the reality of persistent separation and inequality has bred disillusionment and exhaustion among many who personally believe in integrated schools and communities. Faced with stubborn separatist realities, a large number of educational justice advocates have returned to the always-and-still-betrayed promise of the segregationist 1896 *Plessy v. Ferguson* decision: "separate but equal" (though we shall see that conventional educational equity wisdom currently reduces the promise to "separate but adequate"). In place of what appear to them as futile efforts to achieve racial balance in the schools, a growing cadre of black and white liberal educators, activists, and policymakers push for "better-trained and better-paid teachers in urban schools, new buildings, more computers and science labs, and more rigorous standards in math or language skills," charter schools, and/or "magnet schools with specialized programs and the expansion of the Teacher Corps of highly motivated college graduates"—all, Peter Irons notes, within a context of apparently permanent, irreversible, and, in fact, deepening segregation.[5] Numerous newfangled school "reform" and "restructuring" proposals are advanced and implemented, with consequences that are not always clear to even the most trained observers, as part of what the eloquent veteran educational justice witness and writer Jonathan Kozol calls "the 12 ways to be a better apartheid school."[6]

Some dissatisfied "reformers" and black leaders appear to have given up on public education (integrated or not) altogether, embracing the not-so "conservative" right's "market-based" schemes for the siphoning off of public school dollars to fund private school vouchers. The false voucher "solution" means a further weakening of the already under-funded, under-equipped, and disproportionately minority public schools and a strengthening of private schools, whose relatively unaccountable managers are considerably freer than are their public-school counterparts to choose who they admit and serve on the basis of numerous criteria that tend to discriminate against children of color.

Segregated Schools: Race, Class, and Educational Apartheid in Post-Civil Rights America surveys persistent American educational race apartheid in the late twentieth and early twenty-first centuries. The first chapter, titled "Still and Increasingly

Separate," paints a portrait of contemporary, recently rising racial segregation in American schools. It traces the historical evolution of segregated schooling in the United States, the initial post-*Brown* victories and accomplishments of American public-educational desegregation, and the confluence of social, economic, political, legal, and ideological developments that have blocked and rolled back the struggle for racially integrated schools during the last three decades.

The second chapter, titled "Still Savage School Inequalities," shows how the United States' generally regressive method of financing public education works to feed educational disparities between white and minority children. At the same time, it shows that school funding disparities are only the tip of the iceberg of racial-educational disparity. The full phenomenon includes critical differences in teacher quality, teacher stability, curriculum, school materials, teacher expectations, school facilities, student-teacher ratios, discipline and drop-out policies, pedagogy, and more.

The third chapter, titled "Separate But Adequate: The Campaign for Fiscal Equity" describes the history, accomplishments, limits, and persistent legitimacy of the state-level movement for fiscal equity that has arisen and won various notable victories in the United States since the 1970s.

The book's fourth and longest chapter is titled "The Deeper Inequality." It describes the terrible impact that heavily racialized, highly concentrated socioeconomic disadvantage has on the educational experience of many minority students. Arguing that inequality of socioeconomic condition is itself inequality of educational opportunity, this chapter demonstrates how broad class and racial inequalities interact to negatively effect black and Latino learning in ways that fall significantly beyond the reach of schools and educational policy. It treats the academic literature and debates that have arisen in connection with the powerful influence of extra-school factors—primarily concentrated poverty and racial isolation—on educational equity. It defends those who emphasize the role of these factors against the charge of educational "fatalism" and pessimistic "determinism." In making schools their only focus, I argue, many educational reformers needlessly, mistakenly, and, in fact, fatalistically neglect the critical role that broader, heavily racialized socioeconomic inequality plays in crippling the educational experience of minority inner-city children.

The fifth and final chapter, "Why Separatism Matters," poses the critical question of why racial separatism matters and addresses the issue of whether meaningful school integration has ever been tried in the United States. It also engages the authoritarian interpretation of supposedly successful "No Excuse" apartheid schools put forth by right wing educational "reformers." It shows how reactionaries selectively choose and interpret educational evidence to support their claim that urban minority educational dilemmas can be meaningfully addressed without the commitment of significantly increased public resources and the expansion of broad social and economic equality for urban minority schools and communities. It offers a detailed critique of the school voucher movement and argues that the largely disappointing results of recent efforts to create "effective" "high-quality" segregated schools are predictable within a larger and all-too unacknowledged framework of educational and societal race and class apartheid, a framework whose oppressive character is deepened by the interrelated ascendancies of neoliberalism, neoconservatism, and neoimperialism. It concludes by advancing broad principles and specific solutions toward the creation of the intimately interrelated goals of social and educational justice and reform in the post-*Brown* era.

1

STILL AND INCREASINGLY SEPARATE

Different races aren't getting to see what each race is about. When they go into the real world, they don't know how to interact with each other.

—Jarod Arvitt, Greenfield, Mississippi, 2003[1]

Something is different about the children gazing out of the windows of the yellow school buses lumbering up Selwyn Elementary School's driveway: most of the black faces are gone.

—*Education Week*, 2004[2]

Affirmative action may well be the only tool left with the potential to ameliorate the negative effects of a college applicant's prior twelve years of segregated schooling. Sit in classrooms, eat in lunchrooms, romp in playgrounds and wander the hallways in randomly selected public schools:

it's right here in the nation's increasingly segregated and astonishingly unequal schools where one finds the most convincing case for keeping affirmative action intact. For more and more high school students, a college campus like Michigan's would provide their first chance to interact, learn, work, even just walk around in a multiracial environment that approximates the American society they'll soon join.

—Gary Orfield and Susan Eaton, 2003[3]

STILL SEPARATE

Chicago 2004

On the morning of Monday, May 10, 2004, I awoke to pick up the prestigious keynote speaker for a Chicago conference I had been directed to organize on the lessons and legacy of the *Brown v. Board of Education* decision. The gathering's purpose was to gauge how to best understand and to act upon the lessons of *Brown* and its aftermath for the task of providing today's children of color with equal educational opportunity. A number of leading researchers and academics and two key local policymakers were scheduled to appear.

As I rushed to the downtown hotel where my speaker was staying, children in Chicago and that city's broader metropolitan area—home to 265 local jurisdictions and more than 200 local school districts—were making their way to schools whose racial composition mocked the spirit of *Brown* and the great civil rights movement that *Brown* helped spark. Nearly fifty years to the day after the highest court in the land ruled that "separate" was "unequal" and thirty-eight years after Martin Luther King, Jr. led giant demonstrations against school segregation in Chicago, the black-white school "segregation index" for the Chicago metropolitan area was 84. This meant that 84 percent of the black children in the six-county Chicago region would have to switch schools for African American children to be evenly distributed throughout the area's schools.

The black school "isolation index" in the metropolitan area was 78, meaning that the average black public school student attended a school that was 78 percent black. According to quantitative segregation analysts' "exposure index," the average black public school student in the Chicago area attended a school that was just 6 percent white and 1.4 percent Asian. Black students were considerably more segregated within the metropolitan area's public schools than any other racial or ethnic group.

In part, these numbers reflected a stark division between predominantly white suburban schools and very predominantly black and minority central city public schools. Of the 211,999 black children enrolled in public schools in the metropolitan area in 2000, 156, 536 (74 percent) attended the Chicago Public Schools (CPS). Of the city's 438,589 public school students in 2002, just 40,350 (9 percent) were white. As *Brown's* anniversary approached, the city's public school authorities had been arguing for some time that the CPS no longer captured enough white students to justify the federal desegregation consent decree it had been operating under for more than two decades.

Within Chicago, the black-white segregation index was 88 percent and the average black public school student attended a school that was 86 percent black. Fifty-four percent of black Chicago public school students attended schools that did not possess a single white student. *Two hundred and seventy-four schools, equaling nearly half (47 percent) of the city's 579 public elementary and high schools (excluding the small number for which race data are unavailable) were 90 percent or more African American and 173 of those schools—30 percent of all public schools in the city—were 100 percent black.* Just 112 or 19 percent of the city's public schools were technically "integrated" (15–70 percent white) and just 57 (10 percent) were a third or more white. More than half (51 percent) of the city's schools were "predominantly black" by the city's definition (set by the aforementioned desegregation decree) of 70 percent and above.[4]

Meanwhile, the average suburban Chicago area white student attended a school that was 86 percent white and just 5 percent black (compared to 15 percent in the central city). Three of every four black schoolchildren in the Chicago area suburbs would have had to switch schools to be evenly distributed throughout the suburban public schools. Only two of the area's top 20 suburban African American school districts (in terms of absolute numbers) were shared with the top 20 white school districts.

The metropolitan area's school segregation measures would have been higher if private school enrollment were included. In 2000, less than half (46.36 percent) of Chicago's school-age white children attended the city's public schools, compared to 88 percent of their black counterparts and 85 percent of the city's Latino children.[5]

Public School Segregation at the National Level

The Chicago metropolitan area is one of the most racially segregated urban regions in the United States, but its numbers are hardly off the national school segregation charts. As Leonard Steinhorn and Barbara Diggs-Brown note in their book *By the Color of Our Skin: The Illusions of Integration and the Reality of Race*, "just as our neighborhoods are separated by race, so too are our schools. Millions of black children attend schools with few or no whites. Millions more white children attend schools with few or no blacks. Whites rarely constitute more than 15 percent of the students in our nation's largest urban school districts, and most of the time they attend predominantly white schools in their own corner of the city."[6]

Of 1.1 million children attending the New York City public schools in 2004, just 15 percent were white. Thirty-two percent of the city's students were black and 40 percent were Latino. The "population of many [New York City] schools," noted Gail Robinson on the day of *Brown*'s fiftieth anniversary, was "even more skewed than the student population as a whole." *Sixty percent* of all black students in New York City attended schools that were *at least 90 percent black.*[7]

The average U.S. white public school student in 1999–2000 attended a school that was nearly four-fifths (78 percent) white, less than one-tenth (9 percent) black, and just 8 percent Hispanic. By contrast, the average African American student's school was 57 percent black. Latino kids were heavily concentrated in majority Latino schools. The nation's public schools were 62 percent white, but just more than a fourth (28 percent) of the average black student's schoolmates were white. The national black-white school segregation index was quite high at 65.[8]

According to the Harvard Civil Rights Project in 2003, one-sixth of the United States' black public school students attend virtually all nonwhite schools. Just one seventh of the white students attend "multiracial" schools, defined as those with a minority enrollment of 10 percent or higher.[9] By the calculations of leading desegregation researcher Charles Clotfelter, more than a third (37.4 percent) of the nation's black students in 2000 attended schools that were 90 to 100 percent nonwhite in 2000 and nearly three-fourths (72 percent) attended schools that were at least 50 percent nonwhite. In the Northeast and Midwest, the share of black students in 90–100 percent minority schools was 51 and 46 percent, respectively.[10]

Throughout the nation, blacks are disproportionately concentrated and often provide the majority element in big city school districts that are surrounded by predominantly white suburban communities and school districts. Nearly one-third (32 percent) of the nation's black and Hispanic public school students attend what the Department of Education designates a "large city" (a central city with a population of 400,000 or more) school district, whereas just 6 percent of all white students in the United States are enrolled in such districts. More than half (51 percent) of the nation's black public school students are concentrated in large or mid-size cities; the comparable statistic for white students is 17 percent.[11]

By 1998, Steinhorn and Diggs-Brown report that less than 4,000 white students remained in the Atlanta public schools. In Atlanta, as throughout big-city America, there are very few white kids left to integrate with. Nationally, black students are three times as likely as whites to attend urban school systems, which happen, contrary to the common perception, to be considerably more segregated than their rural counterparts. The lion's share of relevant racial school segregation takes places *between* and not *within* school districts, reflecting division between the nation's "chocolate cities and vanilla suburbs" and—of rising significance during the last two decades—between black suburbs and white suburbs.[12]

Private Schools and the "Dual System of De Facto Segregation"

Meanwhile, there is considerable race segregation between disproportionately minority public schools and disproportionately white private schools. In "community after community," Steinhorn and Diggs-Brown note, "the story is the same: blacks make up a significantly larger proportion of [public, P.S.] school children than their percentage of the school-age population." Large numbers of whites leave the public school system for private schools "when the black student population inches above the token."[13]

The racialized public-private split is sharply evident in the flatlands of the Mississippi Delta. In 2000, private schools enrolled more than half of all white students in forty-one nonmetropolitan deep Southern counties concentrated in Mississippi, Alabama, and Georgia; the very same areas where "Jim Crow" segregation had been enforced with special rigidity prior to the *Brown* decision. In one such jurisdiction, Mississippi's Washington County, blacks made up 65 percent of total population but whites comprised 85 percent of private school enrollment and just 13 percent of the public schoolchildren. Thanks to a "dual system of de facto segregation," the Associated Press (AP) reported in the spring of 2003, "the era of [school] segregation never really ended" in the Delta.

A perfect example was found in Greenville, Mississippi, home to three very predominantly white private school academies. At one such academy, the AP found, "357 children start each day with a prayer and a bible reading. Just three of them are black...Less than a mile away, at public Western High School, Jarod Arvitt is an honor student and editor of the campus newspaper. He's one of only four whites out of 526 students." Arvitt, who rejected his parents' offer to send him to a private school, told the AP that Greenville's apartheid system means that "different races aren't getting to see what each race is about" in Greenville's segregated schools. "When they go into the real world," Arvitt commented, "they don't know how to interact with each other."[14]

Inside Schools

At the same time, strong racial segregation persists *inside* nominally integrated schools. As Steinhorn and Diggs-Brown note, "we like to think of racially balanced schools as integrated, but they are not. Race [remains]...the central organizing principle at these schools, often determining the social and educational lives of the students. Youngsters of both races may pass each other and even talk a bit in the hall, but their contact in the lunchroom, the classroom, and the schoolyard is frequently defined by race." Race's role as the leading coordinating "principle" inside racially mixed schools emerges especially after the elementary grades. It begins in middle school and "ossifies" in high school, "when students become acutely conscious of what it means to—as they put it—act one's color."[15]

In the first and only large-scale national study of intra-school segregation, conducted during the early 1980s, educational researchers P. R. Morgan and James McPartland found notable intra-school race separatism within a sample of 44,000 U.S. schools. Among high schools that were 70 to 89 percent white, they found that more than 1 in 20 classrooms were less than 10 percent white. More recently, in 2001, educational researchers Charles Clotfelter, Helen Ladd, and Jacob Vigodor found that separation inside schools accounted for a significant share of overall public school segregation in North Carolina. In the tenth grade, they discovered that such intra-school segregation created 57 percent of total black-white segregation in the state's metropolitan areas. "Even in racially integrated public high schools," Clotfelter observed, "classes typically differed in racial composition. Black students were less likely to be assigned to advanced or honors classes and more likely to be assigned to special education tracks for the mentally retarded than white students."[16] Racial separatism inside schools holds no small significance for any assessment of *Brown's* legacy "over the course of a student's school day," Clotfelter noted, "interracial contact has more to do with conversations and encounters in hallways, classrooms, and after-school activities than it does with the school's overall racial composition."[17]

Desegregating a school in terms of its overall racial composition, it would appear, is a necessary but in itself insufficient condition for the creation of a genuinely integrated school environment.

UNEVEN PROGRESS IN TIME AND SPACE

Southern Story

However, this is not to say that progress on the path to school desegregation has not taken place during the half century after

Brown, even though there has not been a single year since *Brown* in which more than 36 percent of the nation's black children attended majority white schools. But significant integrationist transformation is clear when the present is compared with the pre- and early *Brown* era, when fully 40 percent of the nation's schoolchildren lived in states that practiced or had just recently practiced legal educational race-apartheid. "Before *Brown*," Gary Orfield and Chungei Lee note, "virtually all black students in the Southern and Border states were in completely segregated schools. Today, the vast majority are not" and "we are nowhere near the situation that existed in seventeen of our states and the nation's capital 50 years ago, before the civil rights revolution." Between 1960 and 2000, the percentage of black students attending 90 to 100 percent nonwhite public schools in the U.S. fell from at least two-thirds to a little more than one-third (37.4).[18]

But this long-term movement toward racial balance in American public schools has never been smooth or consistent across time or space. Integrationist progress was most dramatic in leading the initial desegregation battlegrounds in the South and the Border states. The percentage of blacks attending very predominantly (90 percent or more) nonwhite public schools fell from 100 to 31 in the South and from 59 to 40 in the Border states during the last four decades of the twentieth century. But the percentage of blacks attending such schools actually *rose* by 11 points (from 40 to 51) in the Northeast and fell only modestly (from 56 to 46) in the Midwest. In the West, always the nation's least segregated region, the percentage rose from 27 to 30.[19]

In regional terms, then, post-*Brown* public school desegregation has been most particularly *a southern story*, consistent with Martin Luther King Jr.'s observation in the middle 1960s that anti-black racism was actually most intractable and intense in the sprawling metropolises of the North, where *de facto* segregation kept the races nearly as separate and unequal as the *de jure* segregation of the South. More than thirty years after King's assassination, indeed, it's the northern Midwest and Northeast—to which large African American populations migrated in flight from Southern segregation and racism in the twentieth century—that leap off the statistical tables as the most educationally segregated sections of the nation, concentrating a significantly greater share of black children in very predominantly minority schools than either the Border states or the South. By black-white dissimilarity measures, the North was home to 18 of the 20 most public school-segregated metropolitan areas and 42 of the 50 most segregated metropolitan areas in the nation in 2000 (see Table 1.1). Among the nation's 20 leading metropolitan areas for absolute number of black schoolchildren, moreover, northern regions show significantly greater black-white segregation than southern or Border regions.

In noting the vanguard role of the South, it should be recognized that school desegregation there required considerable courage on the part of black students, parents, and their civil rights allies. The *Brown* decision was resisted with ferocity in the Deep South, where top political officials like Arkansas Governor Orval Fabus and Alabama Governor George Wallace gave voice to the deep roots of anti-black racism in the psyches of southern whites, including those of the southern white lower class, for whom racism had long provided what the great black intellectual W.E.B. DuBois called "a public and psychological wage." "Jim Crow" segregation and slavery had given poor Southern Caucasians a measure of status and privilege that was used "to make up for alienating and exploitative class relationships. White workers could and did," as David Roediger has noted, "define and accept their [subordinate] class position by fashioning identities as 'not slaves' and 'not blacks.'"[20]

"Even a dozen years after the Supreme court's decision holding racial segregation in state-run facilities unconstitutional,"

Table 1.1 Top 20 Metropolitan Areas for Black Public School Enrollment

Metropolitan Area (Region)	Black–White Dissimilarity 2000	Black–White Dissimilarity 1990	National Ranking for Black–White Dissimilarity (2000)
New York, NY (N)	80.6	79.8	10 of 329
Chicago (N)	83.9	83.2	2
Atlanta (S)	68.2	68.0	63
Washington, DC (B)	66.6	65.0	75
Detroit (N)	88.5	88.7	1
Philadelphia (N)	74.8	74.5	24
Houston (S)	70.2	63.6	52
Los Angeles (W)	66.8	69.5	71
Baltimore (B)	72.8	74.1	34
Dallas (S)	62.1	62.5	98
Memphis (B)	72.7	68.2	35
St. Louis (B)	69.6	67.4	58
New Orleans (S)	71.3	66.5	42
Norfolk-Virginia Beach, and Newport News, VA (S)	46.3	43.6	217
Miami (S)	72.2	68.5	37
Cleveland (N)	81.2	77.4	8
Ft. Lauderdale (S)	60.9	61.6	106
Charlotte-Gastonia (S)	45.9	36.6	221
Raleigh-Durham (S)	37.6	32.3	281
Newark, NJ (N)	82.3	85.2	3

Note: (N) = North, (S) = South, (B) = Border states, (W) = West. Source: Lewis Mumford Center for Comparative Urban and Regional Research, School Segregation, 1990–2000 (http://mumford.albany.edu/census/index.asp).

notes Derrick Bell, "legions of whites in the deep South determined, often violently, that the court's desegregation orders would never be enforced. For them, separate and unequal was more than a racial policy, it was a self-defeating narcotic under the influence of which even the lowliest white person could feel superior." By the recollections of Bell, himself a former leading civil rights lawyer who litigated southern desegregation cases during the early 1960s, the threat of racist intimidation and violence hung in the air constantly for desegregation law-yers and their clients. People who dared to challenge Southern school segregation became "special objects of hated by whites and persons to be avoided by many but, thank goodness, not all blacks." Recalling one case in Leake County, Mississippi, Bell relates, "the always-hostile white opposition...turned ugly. Nightriders came through [the black community of] Harmony [Mississippi] firing guns into homes." Many of the 52 black par-ents who initially signed a desegregation petition against the Leake County School Board "lost their jobs, or had their credit cut off by merchants. Before long, only fifteen names were left on the petitions."[21]

White resistance in Dixie also took less violent forms. Southern school officials responded to *Brown* by introducing "freedom of choice plans" that permitted parents to select the "whitest" available schools for their children and "majority-mi-nority plans" to let parents move their children "from schools in which they are a racial minority to those in which their race formed a majority." One popular technique used by many dis-tricts to avoid integration was to pass "pupil placement laws" that let school boards use various segregationist "suitability criteria" in assigning students to public schools. In one noto-rious case, that of Prince Edward County in Virginia, school officials responded to a Supreme Court desegregation order by closing their public schools altogether. As nearly all the county's white students enrolled in the private Prince Edwards Academy (staffed by teachers from the closed public schools), the county's black students had *no schools to attend* between 1959 and 1963.[22]

At the same time, school segregation before and after *Brown* was maintained quite effectively outside the South without for-mal legal separation and open violence. Separate and unequal schooling was imposed in northern states and cities through residential segregation and various school-related policies, including the purposeful construction of new schools in all or nearly all-white locations, the racial gerrymandering of school attendance zones, the expansion of black enrollment in majority black schools (often through the use of portable classrooms), and the use of "liberal transfer policies" to ease white movement out of excessively "colored" schools.[23] It should also be noted that the region where *Brown* had the greatest impact on the racial makeup of the public schools—the South—"was also the region with the largest increase in private school enrollment" after the decision. In the rural South, Clotfelter notes, "private schools became the vehicle for the virtual abandonment of public schools in some counties with high proportions of nonwhite students."[24]

White Resistance and Civil Rights Revolution, 1954–1980

Two prominent facts merit special attention in considering the historical pace and path of school integration. The first striking thing about desegregation's time-plotting is the remarkable concentration of its most dramatic advance in the late 1960s and early 1970s. The Border states and Washington, D.C. moved "quickly and quietly" toward desegregation in the middle and late 1950s, reducing the percentage of blacks in 90–100 percent nonwhite schools from 100 to 59 between 1954 and 1961. But there was almost no measurable decline in school segregation in the South between the *Brown* decision and the middle 1960s. Ten years after *Brown*, just *one fiftieth* of Southern black children attended integrated schools in the South. And northern segregation remained essentially unaltered through the mid-1970s.[25]

After practically zero progress between 1954 and 1964, however, Southern desegregation picked up speed during the mid-1960s and leaped forwarded at a practically revolutionary pace during the late 1960s and early 1970s. From 1969 to 1972, in fact, black-white contact in Southern public schools rose dramatically. The share of Southern black public school students attending 90–100 percent nonwhite schools fell from 4 in every 5 (78 percent) to 1 in 4 (25 percent) between 1968 and 1972. Nationally, the comparable decline during the same years was from 64.3 to 38.7 percent.[26]

The radical escalation of desegregation's pace during these years reflected political and legal developments related to the escalation of the civil rights movement and the spread of racial conflict during the 1960s. The *Brown* ruling was really two decisions, neither of which came close to ending segregation in any substantive or reasonably rapid way. After abolishing formal educational race separatism in a pure legal sense on May 17, 1954, the original *Brown* ruling failed to say precisely how or when southern schools were to be concretely desegregated. The high court merely asked the litigants to come back with advice on how and when corrections and remedies might be implemented.

One year later, in "*Brown II*," the court rendered an extremely cautious decision that refused to provide either a timetable or an actual plan to the fix the problem of separate and unequal schools. It required only that southern schools overcome legal public-educational race apartheid with "all deliberate speed." Most of the racist white South took this to mean that it was free to stall and resist with impunity and acted accordingly over the next ten years. At the same time, the *Brown* ruling was initially understood to apply only to the South and to hold no relevance for the North, where de jure (legal and state-mandated) segregation was not practiced but de facto race segregation was widespread.

Things began to change dramatically, however, during the 1960s. Along with well-known provisions eliminating segregated public accommodations, the Civil Rights Act of 1964 authorized the U.S. Department of Justice to initiate federal action suits against legally segregated school districts. It authorized the U.S. Department of Health, Education and Welfare to withhold federal funds from such districts, a threat that took on great significance after the 1965 Elementary and Second Education Act created a large pot of new federal funding for school districts.

Four years later, as the nation erupted in racial violence, the Supreme Court ruled in *Green v. County School of New Kent County* that schools have an "affirmative duty" to totally desegregate and defined desegregation as the elimination of "identifiably white" and "identifiably black" schools. *Green*, notes Gary Orfield, "ordered root and branch eradication of segregated schooling and specified several areas of a school system—such as students, teachers, transportation, and facilities—in which desegregation was mandatory."[27] *Green* said that the attainment of a "unitary" school system—meaning discrimination-free, equal, and fully integrated integration—was the ultimate and permanent goal of *Brown*. Any school district practice or policy that worked against this goal, leading back to a "dual system," was impermissible under *Green*.[28]

In 1969, the high court ruled in *Alexander v. Holmes County* [Mississippi] *Board of Education* that "dual" (segregated) school systems be transformed "at once" and "hereafter" into "unitary" systems. The vague "all deliberate speed" time frame had finally and officially expired.

Two years later, in *Swann v. Charlotte-Mecklenberg Board of Education,* the court struck down student assignment plans that produced racially separate schools by relying on segregated residential patterns. *Swann* approved cross-town busing as a means for districts to become unitary.

And in *Keyes v. Denver School District No. 1* (1973), finally, the Court ruled against de facto school segregation in the North and West, where no states explicitly mandated racial segregation in public schools. The *Keyes* decision held districts responsible for policies that produced such segregation, including the gerrymandering of school attendance zones and the construction of schools in racially isolated neighborhoods. Under *Keyes*, an entire district was illegally segregated when even just one portion of that district was found to be intentionally segregated.

The *Green, Alexander, Swann,* and *Keyes* decisions ushered in an era of local voluntary and federal court-ordered desegregation plans that moved many hundreds of thousands of students into new schools. As Charles Clotfelter notes, these plans varied according to the history and nature of the segregation that had developed in different locales. "In districts where schools had been segregated by law," Clotftler observes, "a natural path to desegregation was simply to draw boundaries around schools to achieve something akin to neighborhood schools. Where neighborhoods were themselves highly segregated, a condition applying to most big cities and many other large districts, desegregation could be achieved only by rezoning attendance areas, sometimes made possible by closing some schools. One variant of this approach was to pair previously racially identifiable schools so that one school served both schools' students in some grades, say 1–3, while the other school specialized in other grades, say 4–6." Other methods included the use of open enrollment to separate school assignments from segregated attendance boundaries and the development of "magnet schools," which "usually meant putting special programs in downtown locations in hopes of attracting students from suburban locations, and at the same producing racially mixed downtown schools."[29]

As was shown by the explosion of racially tumultuous white protest that ensued in response to federal "forced busing" in South Boston during the 1970s, mass white resistance to school desegregation was hardly restricted to the South. This fierce and highly organized white opposition in the regional cradle of abolitionism seemed to give haunting support to a key segregationist ruling penned by Massachusetts Supreme Court Chief Justice Lemuel Shaw more than *twelve decades* before. In *Roberts v. The City of Boston* (1850), abolitionist lawyer and future U.S. Senator Charles Sumner had argued—making a case not unlike that of the NAACP in 1954—that "the separation of schools...tends to create a feeling of degradation on the part of blacks and of prejudice and uncharitableness in whites." Shaw rejected Sumner's thesis on the psychological damage of segregated schooling, arguing that "the odious distinction of caste, founded in a deep-rooted prejudice in public opinion....is not created by law. Whether these distinctions and prejudice, existing in the opinion and feelings of the community, would not be as effectively fostered by compelling colored and white children to associate together in the same schools, may well be doubted."[30]

"Dismantling Desegregation": The Convenient Myth of Judicial Powerlessness

The second striking thing about the historical ebb and flow of racial school separation since *Brown* is the significant increase in black isolation and segregation that has taken place between the 1980s and the early twenty-first century. After falling steadily during the late 1960s, 1970s, and early 1980s, the percentage of black students attending majority nonwhite (50–100 percent minority) and very (90–100 percent) predominantly nonwhite public schools rose significantly between 1988 and 2001. The increases were quite dramatic in the South, the Border states, and the Midwest (see Tables 1.2 and 1.3).

Of the twenty leading metropolitan areas for total black student population, fifteen experienced an increase in black-white student dissimilarity between 1990 and 2000. "Since the early 1990s," notes the black journalist writer Ellis Cose, "black

Table 1.2 Percentage of Black Public School Students Attending a 50–100 Percent Nonwhite School

Region	1968	1988	1991	2001
South	80.9	56.5	60.1	69.8
Border	71.6	59.6	59.3	67.9
Northeast	66.8	77.3	75.2	78.4
Midwest	77.3	70.1	69.7	72.9
West	72.2	67.1	69.2	75.8

Source: Orfield and Lee (2004)[31]

and Latino children are increasingly likely to find themselves in classes with few if any nonwhite faces. This deepening of black and Hispanic segregation in the public schools took place," Cose observes, "despite the continued growth of integration in other sectors of society."[33] Appropriately enough given segregation's historical strong concentration in the South, the most dramatic increases took place in southern metropolitan areas, including Charlotte (9 point increase in black-white dissimilarity during the 1990s), Houston (6 points), Raleigh-Durham (5 points), and New Orleans (5 points). If the Charlotte area is any indication, black-white segregation has continued to increase in the South since the onset of the twenty-first century. The following account from a 2004 *Education Week* article on "*Brown at 50*" is enough to chill the bones of any true integrationist,

Table 1.3 Percentage of Black Public School Students Attending a 90–100 Percent Nonwhite School

Region	1968	1988	1991	2001
South	77.8	24.0	26.1	31.0
Border	60.2	34.5	34.5	41.6
Northeast	42.7	48.0	49.8	51.2
Midwest	58.0	41.8	39.9	46.8
West	50.8	28.6	26.6	30.0

Source: Orfield and Lee (2004)[32]

especially when we recall that Charlotte was once considered home to the nation's most successful effort at desegregation:[34]

Charlotte, NC

Something is different about the children gazing out of the windows of the yellow school buses lumbering up Selwyn Elementary School's driveway: Most of the black faces are gone.

White children have taken the place of many of the African-American students who were bused to Sewlyn, once an in integrated school in the heart of one of this city's oldest and wealthiest white neighborhoods.

The Charlotte-Mecklenburg school district, free from a federal desegregation order, adopted a colorblind plan for school assignment in 2002 that is producing more racially isolated schools, like Selwyn, and more schools enrolling high concentrations of poor children.

From the mid-1970s through the 1980s, the North Carolina school system made up of Charlotte and surrounding Mecklenburg County earned national acclaim as "the city that made desegregation work." The key was a landmark 1971 ruling by the U.S. Supreme Court in *Swann v. Charlotte-Mecklenburg Board of Education*, that cleared the way for Charlotte—and districts nationwide—to use mandatory busing and race-based student assignment as tools to achieve integration.

Now, many observers wonder whether Charlotte-Mecklenburg's school buses are headed in the right direction. "Charlotte is stumbling and it's falling," laments Roslyn Arlin Mickelson, a professor of sociology at the University of North Carolina at Charlotte. "In a couple of years, in terms of racial composition in the schools, the district is going to back where it was prior to *Swann*."

The 2-year-old plan gives parents a choice of schools and provides all families with spots in the "neighborhood schools" closest to their homes. Since parents overwhelmingly chose their local schools, the district's 148 schools are becoming more racially and socioeconomically unbalanced. Suburban classrooms are overcrowded, and seats are left empty in inner-city schools. Since 2001, Selwyn's black enrollment has decreased by more than half, from 34 percent to 16 percent of its 526 students this year. The percentage of students eligible for free or reduced price lunches, an indicator of family income, fell from 31 percent to 16 percent.

Most of the pupils who left Selwyn now attend schools with large numbers of poor children. Using enrollment figures for 2003-04, Mickelson found that 33 percent of the districts schools were racially balanced, compared...with 51 percent in 2001...the number of schools where the percentage of students receiving free or reduced-price lunches exceeded 50 percent climbed from 53 in 2001 to 76 in 2003

This ongoing increase in racial segregation contrasts sharply with the integrationist spirit of the Supreme Court's decision in the pivotal 2003 *Grutter v. Bollinger* case, which upheld affirmative action in higher education admissions as necessary to meet a "compelling state interest" in maintaining a racially diverse student body. According to the Court, the University of Michigan Law School was correct to argue that student racial diversity produced critical benefits for all students, including enhanced classroom discussion and improved preparation for life in an increasingly multiracial workplace and society.[35]

Part of the successful civil rights defense of affirmative action at Michigan, it is worth noting, included references to high and increasing rates of black public school isolation and segregation in the fifth decade out from *Brown*. "Affirmative action," noted expert witnesses Gary Orfield and Susan Eaton in March 2003, "may well be the only tool left with the potential to ameliorate the negative effects of a college applicants' prior twelve years of segregated schooling. Sit in classrooms, eat in lunchrooms, romp in playgrounds and wander the hallways in randomly selected public schools," Orfield and Eaton wrote in *The Nation*, "It's right here in the nation's increasingly segregated and astonishingly unequal schools where one finds the most convincing case for keeping affirmative action intact. For more and more high school students, a college campus like Michigan's would provide their first chance to interact, learn, work, even just walk around in a multiracial environment that approximates the American society they'll soon join."[36]

What went wrong, from a pro-integration perspective at least, with school desegregation in America? Why, indeed, have schools been moving backward, from "the dream of *Brown*" to the "nightmare of *Plessy*," to use the language of the Harvard Civil Rights Project? According to Brian Jones, general counsel for President George W. Bush's Department of Education in the spring of 2004, "We all have to realize the limitations of what a court case like *Brown* can do. It was a critically important watershed moment in terms of the legal landscape," Jones told the *Chicago Tribune*, "but it has its limits. It's one thing to say you can't segregate your schools by law. But the Supreme Court can't mandate where people choose to live."[37]

Jones' two-pronged explanation—emphasizing the inherently inadequate reach of law and the dominant role of residential segregation in the creation of school segregation —ignores the fact that racial school separatism rose even as racial residential separatism fell during the 1990s. It forgets that federal courts and other federal agencies actively and successfully ordered the desegregation of schools across residential lines during the late 1960s and 1970s. It deletes the important fact that blacks continue to face considerable prejudice and discrimination in U.S. housing markets and therefore remain considerably unable to freely "choose" where they wish "to live"—a problem not without some basis in the agency of law.[38]

Above all, Jones fails to grasp the active and in fact powerful role of U.S. law and its leading authority—the U.S. Supreme Court—in the dismantlement of public school desegregation. The integrationist legal and policy revolution of the 1960s lost momentum under the reactionary rule of Richard Nixon, who appointed four high court justices, including the backward-looking civil rights opponent William Rehnquist, after a Republican presidential campaign that attacked school busing as part of a racist-"backlash" "Southern strategy." In *Milliken v. Bradley* (1974), the first and chief *Brown*-related decision rendered under the Nixon-shaped Supreme Court, the justices blocked inter-district city-suburban desegregation plans except in cases where integration advocates could prove that suburban or state officials had taken specific actions to create racially isolated minority city schools. Since it is extremely difficult to prove such suburban or state liability, *Milliken* made it essentially impossible for public officials to bridge the gap between predominantly white suburban schools and predominantly minority schools.[39] *Milliken* effectively underwrote and even encouraged the heavily racialized city-suburban residential split that Jones treats as beyond the reach of law.

It was a factor behind the fact that the number of white school-age children living in Detroit fell by more than half between 1970 and 1980, when blacks made up three-fourths of the city's school-age population. By 1990, the number of white school-age children left in Detroit was down to less than 35,000. By 1999, 91 percent of Detroit's schoolchildren were blacks while schoolchildren in most Detroit suburbs were nearly all white, with the most affluent districts (Gross Pointe, Livonia, and Farmington Hills) the most lily-white of all.

This demographic story, repeated across the nation since the 1970s, is sadly consistent with then Supreme Court Justice Thurgood Marshall's dissenting opinion in the *Milliken* case. In that opinion, Marshall worried that the *Milliken* ruling would encourage "our great metropolitan areas to be divided up each into two cities—one, white, the other black,"[40] a comment that recalls Martin Luther King, Jr.'s warning in 1967: "I see nothing in the world more dangerous than Negro cities ringed by white suburbs."[41]

Subsequent pivotal high-court decisions reflecting the right-wing bent of predominantly Republican-appointed justices have been no less unkind to the cause of school integration. In *Riddick v. School Board of the City of Norfolk, Virginia* (1986), the court permitted a formerly "unitary" school district to dismantle its desegregation plan and return to local government control. In *Board of Education of Oklahoma v. Dowell* (1991), the court ruled that attainment of "unitary status" permitted a district to reinstitute segregated neighborhood schools. Formerly segregated districts were permitted to drop court-ordered busing even if some school segregation remained, as long as all "practicable" actions to dissolve past discrimination had been undertaken.[42] In *Freeman v. Pitts* (1992), the Court ruled that "school districts partially released from their desegregation responsibilities even if integration had not been achieved in all the specific areas outlined in the *Green* decision."

Since *Dowell*, Derrick Bell notes, federal courts have "taken almost every opportunity to release school districts from court-ordered desegregation, even where a substantial number of racially identifiable schools remain or might emerge." In numerous cases, the courts have used the threat of residential white flight (from black neighbors)—itself encouraged by the court's own *Milliken* ruling—as a reason to dissolve urban desegregation orders.[43]

Diehard integrationists in the post-civil rights era can take some heart, perhaps, from the *Grutter* ruling on affirmative action. But the 2003 decision offers little for the large number of hyper-segregated black primary and secondary students for whom higher education and its benefits are beyond reach. As Henry Giroux and Susan Searls Giroux noted in 2003, *Grutter* provided "little advantage to poor minorities" since "higher education remains out of reach for the vast majority of poor youth, who are subject to grossly inferior and rapidly re-segregating elementary and secondary schools." [44] The *Grutter* decision, it should also be noted, did not uphold affirmative action in the name of racial justice and black educational equality—key principles behind the *Brown* ruling—but largely in support of the notion that predominantly white mainstream American educational and life and work skills quality are enhanced by the experience of racial diversity in higher education.

THE RISE OF THE POST-CIVIL RIGHTS ERA

The Integrationist Conjuncture: 1945–1970

Of course, the key court decisions that have so critically shaped the rise and retreat of school desegregation have been neither promulgated nor enforced in socially and politically autonomous legal-historical vacuums. They have derived their content, purpose, and power from at once broader and deeper social, moral, political, and ideological forces that shifted significantly over the half-century after *Brown*. The *Brown* decision and the subsequent civil rights movement and legislation that was inspired by *Brown* and enabled the ruling's enforcement drew considerable strength from the cold war imperatives of U.S. foreign policy in the 1950s and 1960s. Legal racial segregation, school separatism especially, was embarrassing to U.S. policymakers in a period when widely disseminated

U.S. doctrine maintained that America was the glorious embodiment, homeland, headquarters, guardian, and agent of freedom and democracy in a great global contest with the supposedly expansionist, totalitarian, and evil Soviet Union and its allies in "international communist conspiracy." Concerns over the deleterious impact of domestic U.S. race apartheid on America's ability to win global and especially Third World allegiances were critical to the *Brown* ruling. It was "impossible," as W.E.B. DuBois argued after the decision, "for the United States to continue to lead a 'Free World' with race segregation kept legal over a third of its territory."

DuBois' judgment was consistent with the U.S. Justice Department's *amicus brief* to the *Brown* case. Supporting the NAACP's argument that legally segregated schooling was bad for American global public relations, the department quoted Secretary of State and leading cold war architect Dean Acheson on how "the undeniable existence of racial discrimination [in the U.S.] gives unfriendly governments the most effective kind of ammunition for their propaganda warfare." School segregation, Acheson argued, "remains a constant embarrassment to this government in the day-to-day conduct of its foreign relations," and "jeopardized the efficient maintenance of our moral leadership of the free and democratic nations of the world."[45]

The civil rights movement richly and creatively exploited the tensions between U.S. cold war rhetoric and domestic U.S. racial inequalities to advance the struggle for racial justice. During the middle and late sixties, moreover, the struggle for black equality moved beyond the South to the entire nation. It pushed beyond legal protest and the demand for mere desegregation and voting rights to make an increasingly militant call for substantive black social and political equality and power. The onset of mass racial violence in leading U.S. cities combined with the emergence of mass, predominantly white protest against the racist U.S. war on Vietnam and the emergence of a rebellious, campus-based New Left and youth counter-culture that were significantly inspired by black experience and struggle to press public officials to dismantle race apartheid in America.

"All The Corrections Have Been Made"

"Things," as Bob Dylan sings, "have changed." The global public relations pressure formerly exercised by a relevant "Communist" enemy bloc has long since disappeared, leaving no remotely comparable rival or deterrent state or bloc capable of deriving advantage from American racial contradictions. Also gone is any widespread sense that American race relations are in need of serious, substantive, and reasonably rapid repair. A greater percentage of Americans than ever before tell opinion pollsters that that they believe in the at once racially integrationist and racially egalitarian goals of the now officially mainstream civil rights movement. There is a chasm, however, between these passively declared white values and the reality of white behavior and commitments, seen in routine white flight from neighborhoods and schools that contain any but a small number of black Americans and in white reluctance to support the passage and/or enforcement of basic civil rights laws for open housing, civil rights enforcement, and affirmative action.[46]

This mass white racial indifference feeds on the great post-civil rights illusion that black separateness and inequality have been overcome, a misapprehension that draws on the limited and fading victories of the civil rights movement. For most whites in "post-Civil Rights" America, black-white integration and equality is more than just an accepted ideal. It is also, many believe, an *accomplished reality,* manifested in the high visibility of wealthy and powerful African American personalities like Michael Jordan, Oprah Winfrey, and Colin Powell, the multi-racial composition of broadcast news teams, and the official playing of King's "I Have a Dream" speech on television screens and in schoolrooms across the nation. According to an article in the *Washington Post*, a survey conducted in the spring of 2001 by the newspaper, the Henry J. Kaiser Foundation, and Harvard University found that "large numbers of white Americans incorrectly believe that Blacks are as well off as whites in terms of their jobs, incomes, schools, and health care."[47]

Insofar as racial differences in wealth, income, security and general well being persist between blacks and whites, the large majority of white Americans deny that anti-black racism is the cause. Many whites point to the elimination of numerous discriminatory laws and barriers as well as the passage of equal employment legislation and affirmative action as proof that American society "bent over backwards" to guarantee blacks "equal opportunity." Convinced that racism is no longer a significant problem for blacks, most whites find the real barriers to black success and equality within the African American community itself. If problems for blacks persist, many whites and some privileged blacks (e.g., John McWhorter at the Manhattan Institute) think that it is only because too many blacks engage in "self-sabotaging" behaviors. "As white America sees it," note Steinhorn and Diggs-Brown, "every effort has been made to welcome blacks into the American mainstream and now they're on their own."

Predominant white attitudes at the turn of the millennium are well summarized by the comments of a white respondent to a survey conducted by *Essence* magazine. "No place that I'm aware of," wrote the respondent, "makes [black] people ride on the back of the bus or use a different restroom in this day and age. We got the message; we made the corrections—get on with it." Even among some African American and other intellectuals who describe themselves as "left" and/or "center-left" (most prominently e.g., Harvard's Henry Louis Gates) there is a tendency in the post-civil rights era to question the notion that "race" or, more accurately, racism is a significant reason for the persistently disproportionate presence of blacks at the bottom, and relative absence at the top, of America's socioeconomic, political, and institutional hierarchies.[48]

This conclusion rests on a failure to distinguish adequately between overt and covert societal racism. The first variety has a long and sordid history. It includes such actions, policies and practices as the burning of black homes and black churches, the public use of derogatory racial slurs and epithets, the open banning of blacks from numerous occupations, the open political disenfranchisement of blacks, and the open legal segregation of schools and public facilities by race. This variety is largely defeated, outlawed, and discredited in the United States. Witness, for example, the rapid public humiliation and political demotion of Trent Lott, who lost his position as United States Senate Majority Leader after he spoke in nostalgic terms about the openly segregationist 1948 presidential campaign of Strom Thurmond.

The second variety involves the more impersonal operation of social and institutional forces and processes in ways that "just happen" but nonetheless serve to reproduce black disadvantage in the labor market and numerous other sectors of American life. It includes racially segregating real estate and lending practices, residential white flight, racial discrimination in hiring and promotion, the systematic under-funding and under-equipping of schools predominately attended by blacks relative to schools predominately attended by whites (a key subject matter in the next two chapters of this book), and the disproportionate surveillance, arrest, and incarceration of blacks. Richly enabled by policymakers who commonly declare allegiance to anti-racist ideals, it has an equally ancient history that has outlived the explicit, open and public racism of the past and the passage of civil rights legislation that is justly cherished within and beyond the black community.

Covert racism may actually be deepened by these civil rights victories and related black upward mobility into the middle and upper classes insofar as those victories and achievements have served to encourage the illusion that racism has disappeared and that the only obstacles left to African American success and equality are internal to individual blacks and their community—the idea that, in Derrick Bell's phrase, "the indolence of blacks rather than the injustice of whites explains the socioeconomic gaps separating the races."[49] Indeed, "it's hard," Steinhorn and Diggs-Brown note, "to blame people" for believing—falsely in Steinhorn and Diggs-Brown's view—that racism is dead in America "when our public life is filled with repeated affirmations of the integration ideal and our ostensible progress towards achieving it." In a similar vein, Sheryl Cashin notes that "there are [now] enough examples of successful middle-class African-Americans to make many whites believe that blacks have reached parity with them. The fact that some blacks now lead powerful mainstream institutions offers evidence to whites that racial barriers have been eliminated; the issue now is individual effort . . . the odd black family on the block or the Oprah effect—examples of stratospheric black success—feed these misperceptions, even as relatively few whites live among and interact daily with blacks of their own standing."[50] Episodes and events like the demotion of Trent Lott or the election of a black U.S. Senator (Carol Mosley Braun in 1992 and Barack Obama in 2004) or big city mayoral criticism of, say, racist sentiments on the part of bigoted white firemen, offer opportunities for city, state, and national leaders to pat themselves on their back for advancing beyond the primitive state of level-one racism even while they promote policies that dig the hole of institutional and societal racism yet deeper.[51]

It is interesting to note that Martin Luther King, Jr. sensed some of the danger here at the outset. He noted in 1967 that "many whites hasten to congratulate themselves on what little progress [black Americans] have made. I'm sure," King opined, "that most whites felt that with the passage of the 1964 Civil Rights Act, all race problems were automatically solved. Most white people are so removed from the life of the average Negro, there has been little to challenge that assumption."[52]

From New Deal Era to the Neoliberal Age

White indifference to black reality also feeds on the nation's generation-long working and middle-class wage and salary squeeze and the related collapse of the liberal mid-twentieth century New Deal order. The relative decline of nonaffluent white income and economic security during the decades that followed the 1960s pinnacle of the civil rights movement undercut the white majority's never terribly impressive willingness to share space, resources, power, and sentiments with black and brown others. It has also gravely weakened the critical underlying "liberal consensus" that held political and ideological sway during the 1950s and 1960s. According to one of the key principles underlying that lost consensus, the remarkably and seemingly endless abundance generated by the expansion of world-hegemonic American capitalism made it possible for U.S. policy makers to grant social justice and meet their domestic population's basic needs regardless of race, class, color, and creed, without resort to negative "Marxist" redistributions of wealth and income and nasty "zero-sum" conflicts between different social ranks and groups. A "rising tide" would "lift all boats," admitting everyone to the American Dream without disturbing existing social hierarchies and inequalities of class, race, and power.[53]

This "liberal consensus" conferred a major legitimate role to government in the planning and regulating of economic activity and in distributing resources to reduce the costs of inequality for those at the bottom of the American economic system. It made welfare expenditures, income maintenance, education, child and health care, job training and the like the greatest part of public spending. People engaged in such public "welfare activities" became "the largest body of all public employment. In 1970, while the Vietnam War was at its height," notes Eric Hobsbawm, "the number of school employees in the USA for the first time became significantly larger than the number of military civilians and defense personnel."[54] The nation's large number of education and other workers and professionals from the public sector embodied the liberal welfare-state's commitment to the maintenance of a social contract that guaranteed basic social provisions—including access to adequate education, housing, health care, transportation, and other public services—to the broad populace, including the least advantaged.

With the onset of significant U.S. economic decline and related regressive corporate de-industrialization and restructuring and escalated global capital mobility in the 1970s and 1980s, however, the New Deal consensus was attacked and largely supplanted by the regressive, authoritarian, and overlapping ideologies of corporate neoliberalism and neoconservatism. The first ideology holds that the "free market" and purely private economic rationality are the solution to nearly all social and personal problems. By neoliberal dictates, "The market should be allowed to make major social and political decisions...the state should voluntarily reduce its role in the economy...corporations should be given total freedom...trade unions should be curbed and citizens given much less rather than more social protection."[55] "Wedded to the belief that the market should be the organizing principle for all political, social, and economic decisions," Henry A. Giroux observes:[56]

neoliberalism wages an incessant attack on democracy, public goods, and noncommodified values. Under neoliberalism everything either is for sale or is plundered for profit. Public lands are looted by logging companies and corporate ranchers; politicians willingly hand the public's airwaves over to broadcasters and large corporate interests without a dime going into the public trust;...public services are gutted in order to lower the taxes of major corporations; schools increasingly resemble malls or jails, and teachers, forced to raise revenue for classroom materials, increasingly function as circus barkers hawking everything from hamburgers to pizza parties—that is, when they are not reduced to prepping students to get higher test scores. As markets are touted as the driving force of everyday life, big government is disparaged as either incompetent or threatening to individual freedom, suggesting that power should reside in markets or corporations rather than in governments and citizens...profit-making is [touted as] the essence of democracy...citizenship [is defined as] an energized plunge into consumerism....Political culture [is] increasingly depoliticized as collective life is organized around the modalities of privatization, deregulation, and commercialization...human misery is largely defined as function of personal choices, and human misfortune is viewed as the basis for criminalizing social problems....Democracy becomes synonymous with free markets while issues of equality, social justice, and freedom are stripped of any substantive meanings and used to disparage those who suffer systemic deprivation and chronic punishment.

From a pure neoliberal perspective, it is now essentially dysfunctional and retrograde to argue that poor minority children need integrated and equal public schools. Poor black parents should look to the supposedly benevolent, inherently liberating and democratic market for appropriately private so-lutions to their children's educational problems. The most they should expect from what neoliberals denounce as the inher-ently flawed public-educational sector is the diversion of tax money from misguided efforts to serve the public educational commons to (barely) help rational individual families pay for private tuitions at schools of their free choice.

Neoconservative doctrine adds reactionary nationalism-imperialism, police state enthusiasm, suspicion of cultural modernism, and authoritarian evangelical pseudo-Christian-ity to neoliberalism's worship of the, in fact, heavily subsidized and corporate-dominated free market. By its dictates, it is prac-tically treasonous for citizens and activists to persist in making claims of racial and social justice upon American educational or other institutions. "What," neoconservatism asks with para-noid alarm in the post-9/11 era (a period that has seen Presi-dent George W. Bush's arch-reactionary first education chief, Rod Paige, refer to the National Education Association as "ter-rorists"), "do you actually mean to suggest that this is not the greatest, most equal, and free nation state on the face of this earth—the beacon to the world of the way life should be?"

Under the cover of a false national solidarity that uses a deeply reactionary culture of fear to silence dissent, neoconser-vatism and neoliberalism together have used the "war on terror" as cover to cut programs for the poor, contain public education spending, rollback civil liberties, and implement radically re-gressive tax cuts that grossly favor the wealthiest 1 percent in what was already the industrialized world's most unequal and wealth-top-heavy nation by far. These harshly plutocratic ac-tions are wrapped in dangerously messianic, pseudo-spiritual and nationalistic rhetoric that invokes God, country, "family values" and "moral issues" to camouflage and justify militantly state-capitalist policies that exacerbate inequality at home and abroad.[57]

Black "Integration Exhaustion"

As white America has moved dangerously to the right on school and other social policies in the post-civil rights era, with recent help from 9/11, the black community's support for school integration has waned considerably. To be sure, polling research indicates that American blacks continue to support racially integrated education more strongly than do either whites or Hispanics. According to a survey of 1,258 adults (consisting of 634 nonHispanic whites, 298 blacks, and 282 Hispanics) conducted for *Newsweek* by Princeton Survey Research Associates in January 2004, 89 percent of blacks, 83 percent of Hispanics, and 66 percent of whites think that "increasing racial diversity and integration" in schools is "an important positive goal." Over 60 percent of blacks and Hispanics but less than a third of whites think that "more should be done to integrated schools throughout the nation."

Bearing in mind that *Brown* was never primarily about integration "for its own sake" for most African Americans, it is important to note that "most blacks are no longer convinced that their kids necessarily do better in integrated schools." Fifty-seven percent of the black parents surveyed by the Princeton polling group said that a school's racial mixture makes *no achievement difference* for black children, way up from the 41 percent who said that in 1988.[58] This judgment is undoubtedly a major reason that, as the *Chicago Tribune* noted in a front-page assessment of *Brown's* legacy in May of 2004, the goal of achieving racial balance in public schools had lost much of its allure in the black community. "For many black parents," the *Tribune* reported last year, "integration is no longer as important as the opportunity to provide their children with an education equal to the received by whites—the hope inspired by the *Brown* case 50 years ago."

As Rose Williams told the *Tribune*, "quality of education is most important to me... Diversity is important because when they go out into the world it's not just going to be people like them. But number 1 is quality of education." When interviewed, Williams had a first- and second-grader at the 96 percent black Jefferson School in the far South Side Chicago neighborhood of Riverdale. [59]

Meanwhile, black commentators express and report on "integration exhaustion" in the black community. Many African Americans have become exasperated with the long, expensive, uneven, and now (once again) uphill struggle required to convince the white majority that schools should be racially balanced. A considerable number of leading black intellectuals now seem to think that the fading integrationist dream of *Brown* was something of a dysfunctional chimera. For such thinkers, racial balance is now somewhat beside the point, whether attainable or not, and the real focus of those who care about the proper education of "Jim Crow's children" (as Peter Irons calls today's minority elementary and secondary students) should be on doing whatever it takes to effectively school children of color within a persistently segregated context.

From the perspective of the legendary black law professor and former civil rights desegregation litigator Derrick Bell, *Brown* was an inherently flawed decision that all-too-easily sidestepped both the question of whites' profound racist reluctance to share school space with black children and the issue of equity between white and black schools. Looking back with regret on his early desegregation career, Bell argued in 2004 that a better, more realistic *Brown* decision would have concerned itself not with overthrowing *Plessy's* separatist doctrine but rather with making America's public schools actually live up to *Plessy's* promise of equal if segregated schools. In his book *Silent Covenants: Brown v. Board and the Unfulfilled Hope for Racial Reform* (published in 2004 to mark *Brown's* fiftieth anniversary), Bell concluded that things would have worked out much more positively for black children if the Supreme Court had ruled in 1954 that "*Plessy v. Ferguson* was still the law of the land." A truly useful *Brown* decision, Bell audaciously argued, would have required schools to provide black children with educational resources equal to those received by white children.

Bell's recommendations for "effective schooling in the post-*Brown* era" said nothing about integration. They focused instead on the struggle for racial school funding equity and the creation and expansion of various models of improved black education within highly segregated environments: inner-city "independent schools," charter schools, specialized public schools, vouchers, Catholic schools, and supplemental school programs.[60]

Bell's negative judgment on *Brown* was significantly shared by the esteemed black Harvard law professor Charles Ogletree. In his retrospective 2004 reflection *All Deliberate Speed: Reflections on the First Half-Century of Brown v. Board of Education*, Ogletree began by noting that "the evil that *Brown* sought to eliminate—segregation—is still with us, and the good it ought to put in its place—integration—continues to elude us." While "*Brown* should be celebrated for ending *de jure* segregation in this country," he continued, "far too many African-Americans have been left behind, while only a relative few have truly prospered. For others, short-term gains have been replaced by setbacks engendered by new forms of racism. School districts, briefly integrated, have become re-segregated. Some distinctively African-American institutions have been permanently destroyed and others crippled"—a reference to the role that *Brown* played in undermining historically black colleges and high schools.

Like Bell, Ogletree questioned the wisdom of the Thurgood Marshall NAACP's emphasis on integrating white schools as the essential goal, without proper attention to the distribution of resources between black and white schools. "What message were we sending to our own children," Ogletree asked, "having them leave their neighborhood schools and sending them to white, presumably better schools?"

Ogletree's recommendations for "meeting the educational challenges of the twentieth century" also had little to do with integration, focusing instead on the development of alternative educational institutions designed to more effectively teach predominantly black and poor inner-city students in segregated settings and on the payment of reparations to compensate African Americans for the deep and long-term damage inflicted by slavery, Jim Crow segregation, and other forms of racial oppression and discrimination to this day. [61]

In a somewhat similar vein, black journalist Ellis Cose marked *Brown*'s fiftieth anniversary by observing that "the decision rested on an assumption that simply wasn't true: that once formal, state-mandated segregation ended, 'equal educational opportunities' would be the result. A half century later," Cose concluded, "school segregation is far from dead and the goal of educational equality is elusive as ever." With black school segregation actually rising "since the early 1990s," Cose argued, the struggle for a decent black education had moved well "beyond *Brown*" to embrace initiatives that had little to do with integration per se: "vouchers, privatization, curbs on social promotion, high-stakes testing." Cose wondered if these and other post-*Brown* measures might "be the second phase of *Brown*: a continuation by other means of the battle for access to a decent education by those whom fortune left behind."[62]

Among the three black law professors who marked *Brown*'s half century anniversary with the publication of a major monograph, only Sheryl Cashin, former law clerk to Thurgood Marshall as a Supreme Court justice, felt compelled to defend the ever more elusive goal of integration. And she did so in a book that bore the title *The Failures of Integration* and was more centrally concerned with residential than with educational integration.[63]

In reality, it is worth noting, white racism has long made the African American community understandably ambivalent about educational integration as a policy goal. "The Negro," wrote W.E.B. DuBois in 1935, "needs neither segregated schools nor mixed schools. What he needs is education."[64] Twenty-six years later, in a remark that might surprise those who think that Martin Luther King, Jr. lacked any race-conscious appreciation of the need for blacks to sustain separate black institutions and identity,[65] King expressed early skepticism about the benefits of school integration. "I favor integration on buses and in all areas of public accommodation," King told two Montgomery, Alabama high school teachers. "I am for equality. However, I think integration in our public schools is different. In that setting, you are dealing with the most important asset of an individual—the mind. White people view black people as inferior. A large percentage of them have a very low opinion of our race. People with such a low view of the black race cannot be given free rein and put in charge of the intellectual care and development of our children."[66]

Has integration been tried and proven a failure in the United States, to state a common judgment among those who have become "exhausted" and dissatisfied with the goals and legacy of *Brown*? It is important here to recognize what Godfrey Hodgson in 1976 called the "sharp distinction between desegregation and true integration." By "true integration," Hodgson meant, following the argument of Harvard educational researcher Thomas Pettigrew, "an atmosphere of genuine acceptance and friendly respect across racial lines." "Mere desegregation," Hodgson added, "won't help blacks do better in school until this kind of atmosphere is achieved."[67] It is questionable indeed that such "true integration" has been seriously attempted in the U.S.

Whether such integration can or will ever be achieved is a matter of conjecture and debate; observers like Bell think not. In the meantime, we are left with what might be called the still unresolved *Plessy* question of persistent educational inequality between predominantly black and predominantly white schools. It is to that topic that the following chapter turns.

2

STILL SAVAGE SCHOOL INEQUALITIES

While many schools are delivering a mediocre product that sells their students short, for some children, especially those living in large central cities with high minority populations and heavy concentrations of the poor, the tale is much more tragic. Broad economic changes are putting a higher and higher premium on educational attainment, yet these students languish in decrepit school buildings, where many of the teachers lack the skills and training they should have, the resources to meet their special challenges, and/or the enthusiasm and faith that might once have led them to consider education their mission and not simply their job.

—Jeffrey Henig et al., 1999[1]

There are few areas in which the value we attribute to a child's life may be so clearly measured as the decisions that we make about the money we believe it's worth investing in the education of one person's child as opposed to that of someone else's child.

—Jonathan Kozol, 2000[2]

Of all the developed countries, only two systematically have spent less money on educating poor children than wealthy children. One is South Africa [under apartheid]; the other is the United States.

—Stan Karp[3]

The school is penalized for these kids. We want quality more than quantity. If that means removing dead weight, we will remove dead weight.

—Chicago inner-city high school principal, 2003[4]

In our neighborhood, children aren't being taught to be critical thinkers, so they aren't able to challenge the conditions they face...when students of color display critical thinking, they are looked at as being disrespectful. When our children challenge a teacher in the classroom about educational issues, they often are sent to the Dean's office for disrupting the class.

—Mary Johnson, parent activist
South Gate, California, 2004[5]

There needs to be a common ground. Children are children. They should all have the same opportunities.

—African-American focus-group participant,
Chicago, IL, December 2003[6]

"A SYSTEM OF EDUCATIONAL APARTHEID"

"There Needs to Be a Common Ground"

In the fall and winter of 2003, I was privileged to observe a series of long discussions on educational quality and school funding issues with six focus groups—two with African-Americans and Latinos in Chicago, two with white Chicago-area suburbanites, and two with white "downstate" Illinois residents in Peoria. In each group, the facilitator opened the conversation by asking participants to imagine that they were talking to a parent who was thinking of moving to Illinois and wanted to know about the quality of the state's public schools. "What," the facilitator asked, "would you tell them?"

Regardless of race, ethnicity, or locale, the members of each group gave the same initial answer: "It depends on where you are going to live." The quality of education that an Illinois child receives, all the groups agreed, depends largely on the zip-code in which that child happens to reside. And this critical matter of chance, many participants knew, was strongly linked to a state school-funding system that allocates educational resources largely on the basis of local property wealth.

I was struck by the extent to which the participants grasped this basic policy issue and by the widespread sense, especially strong on the part of the urban "minority" participants, that these inequalities were wrong and deeply unfair to dispropor-tionately black and Hispanic poor children. "There needs," a black female participant from Chicago stated, in simple and elo-quent terms, "to be a common ground. Children are children," she added. "They should all have the same opportunities."[7]

"Conditions for Black Children
That Many White Parents Couldn't Imagine"

The sad extent to which such "common ground" and sameness of opportunities were missing as these discussions took place was evident in a disturbing front-page *Chicago Tribune* story that appeared on May 9, 2004. The article, based on a statewide *Tribune* study undertaken to mark the fiftieth anniversary of the *Brown* decision, was titled "Still Separate, Unequal: Most of Illinois' Black Students Remain in Separate, Inferior Schools."

"Fifty years after a landmark court brought the promise of better schooling for black students," wrote reporters Diane Rado, Darnell Little, and Grace Adujara, "most of Illinois black students are still relegated to segregated and inferior schools." A black Illinois child, the *Tribune* reported, was 40 times more likely than her white counterpart to attend one of the state's 351 "worst of the worst 'academic watch' schools," where "students have failed state tests and other standards for four years in a row." Nearly 40 percent of the state's black children, the paper found, attend such schools.

Students attending majority black schools in Illinois, the *Tribune* noted, were "about six times more likely" than students in white schools to be instructed by teachers who lacked full teacher certification. Majority black grade schools had "larger class sizes and larger enrollments on average," despite research showing "the benefits of smaller and nurturing learning environments, particularly for disadvantaged children." The *Tribune* observed, "The inequities stretch from Chicago to the suburbs to communities across the state, creating *conditions for black children that many white parents couldn't imagine*" [emphasis added]:

> At the dimly lit Coolidge Middle School in south suburban Phoenix, the library is spacious but it has just eight bookshelves, some half-empty. Administrators at the cash-strapped school haven't been able to buy more library materials for their students, most of them black.
>
> Poor black children file into classrooms where as many as 32 pupils are taught at Price Elementary in Chicago, because too few teachers want to work at a failing school. Less qualified teachers working without credentials help beef up the staff.
>
> In East St. Louis, bars cover windows and metal cages cover air-conditioning units to protect against theft at the deteriorated, all-black Lincoln Middle School. The school's

library has become a refuge, with the staff providing teddy
bears that troubled children can hug....

"I think," Northwestern University professor Alfred Hess, Jr.
told the *Tribune*, "*we have a system of educational apartheid* in
Illinois." [emphasis added][8]

A system, Hess might have added, that tends to spend less
per student on African-American and other minority children
than on white children. In early 2004, the Education Trust,
a leading national school policy and research organization,
ranked the fifty states for school funding equity (or lack there-
of) according to two measures: (1) the per-student funding
gap between each state's top 25 percent and bottom 25 percent
of school districts in terms of child poverty; (2) the same gap
between each state's top 25 percent and bottom 25 percent in
terms of minority representation among children.

By the first measure, the Trust found, Illinois led the United
States in disparity. In 2001, the Trust reported, Illinois spent
an average of $2,834 more per student on children in the least
poor quartile of its districts than on children in its most impoverished quartile. This critical funding disparity translated
into a revenue difference of $953, 600 between two typical Il-
linois elementary schools with 400 students—one composed of
students in a wealthy district and the other in a poor district.

By the second measure—the minority school funding gap—
Illinois ranked seventh in terms of inequity. The state spent an
average of $1,352 more per student on children in the least mi-
nority quartile of districts than on children in its most minor-
ity-based districts. This translated into a revenue difference of
$540,800 between two typical state elementary schools with
400 students—one in a predominantly white district and the
other in a predominantly minority district. No wonder Illinois
was the one state to receive a failing grade for school-funding
equity in the national 2003 report card of the prestigious education journal *Education Week*.[9]

The Hidden Injuries of Race and Class: A Governor's Speech

None of this racially disparate funding inequity appeared to have dented the mind or the heart of the state's nominally "Democratic" and Chicago-based Governor Rod Blagojevich at the beginning of 2004. In his January 2004 State of the State Address, delivered to the Illinois Legislative Assembly, Blagojevich moved quickly into a passionate attack on the state's failing educational system. "I am not satisfied with the state of education in Illinois," Blagojevich said. "While Illinois is blessed with thousands of good schools" and "with tens of thousands of smart, committed, dedicated teachers," he intoned, "our education system is still failing too many children." Blagoejevich recited horrible statistics from the depressing world of standardized testing: "38 percent of [Illinois] kids in the third grade can't read at the third grade level; 36 percent of eight graders do not meet eighth grade reading standards; 41 percent of eighth graders cannot write on an eighth grade level; 44 percent of eleventh graders can't meet basic reading standards; and 48 percent of eleventh grade students taking the ACT exam are not ready for college without having to repeat classes."

Of special concern to the governor was the terrible fact (for him), repeated throughout his address, that only 46 cents of every Illinois education dollar went to classroom instruction. Illinois ranked sixteenth in the nation, he noted, in the amount of money its taxpayers invest in total per-pupil spending. "But when it comes to how we spend that money, Illinois ranks only fortieth in the nation when it comes to seeing that money invested in the classroom to teach our children. *Fortieth in the nation!* Thirty-nine other states do a better job than we do when it comes to how much money makes it into the classroom. By comparison, California, for all of its problems, does a better job than we do. The Golden State spent 3 percent of their education dollars on classroom instruction. Pennsylvania: 54 percent. New York: 60 percent on classroom instruction. The children deserve better," Blagojevich proclaimed. "The parents deserve better. The taxpayers deserve better."

"If we are really serious about fixing our schools," the governor insisted, then Illinois must make "real, fundamental, systemic changes in the way we manage our schools, in the way we spend our education dollars, and in the way we hold people accountable for results." Illinois citizens and policymakers must break their attachment to the wrongheaded notion that "we're not spending enough money" on education. They should embrace, rather, structural reform in *how existing education dollars are spent*.[10]

Nowhere in his speech did Blagojevich show any understanding of the fact that children benefit significantly from numerous educational investments that do not go directly into classroom instruction—school heating systems, lunch programs, lead paint removal, transportation, and so on.[11] And nowhere in his passionate call for "systemic change" in "the way we spend our education dollars" or in his rant about negative inter-state school spending comparisons did he show the slightest appreciation of the fact that Illinois possessed the nation's greatest average school-funding gap between the least and the most impoverished school districts and one of the nation's largest school-funding gaps between high-minority and low-minority school districts.

Given these critical omissions, it was hardly surprising that Blagojevich also displayed a completely class- and color-blind conception of exactly which students Illinois education was most especially "failing." In another unflattering inter-state contrast omitted from his indignant oration, Illinois possessed the nation's largest student test-score gap between wealthy and impoverished students. A recent report available at the time Blagojevich delivered the speech showed that poor kids were especially victimized by the state's failure to provide adequate education, as measured by the admittedly problematic (see below) and routine measure: standardized test scores. Less than half of the state's children who came from low-income amilies, this report showed, met the standards set by the state's testing regimen, meaning that nearly 400,000 nonaffluent Illinois boys and girls were "struggling in school." About 30,000 out of 40,000 eleventh-grade students from low-income families do not meet state standards in mathematics and science. In the state's Prairie State Examination (PSE), just 17.3 percent of students in high-poverty schools met the state's basic math standards. For the PSE as a whole, the report noted, "20.5 percent of students in the high poverty schools meet or exceed state standards compared to almost 57 percent of students in schools enrolling fewer than half of their students from low-income families. Just 6.25 percent of high poverty high schools have half the students meeting PSE standards compared to 73.6 percent of the other high schools."[12]

Another gubernatorial omission comes as no surprise: the *racial and ethnic* achievement gap. In citing test scores as the critical evidence that public schools were failing Illinois children, Blagojevich neglected to mention that black and Latino children were especially shortchanged by his test-based measure of school performance. In 2002, just 32 percent of the state's black students and 26 percent of its Hispanic students met or exceeded state reading standards, compared to 66 percent of white students. The gap was worse in math. These disparities were, in turn, related to numerous other racial and ethnic gaps—steep unemployment, poverty, the availability health care, incarceration and felony marking-disparities, to name just a few, disparities that exist throughout the nation as well as in Illinois—that did not make it into the governor's State of the State address.[13]

THE PROMISE OF *PLESSY*
The Separate But Equal Myth

Of course, Blagojevich's address was hardly the first time that a leading American public official spoke of educational fairness while ignoring harsh fiscal inequities between black and white schools. For an earlier example, we can look, curiously enough, at the *Brown* decision itself.

The great lie at the heart of the segregationist legal doctrine that *Brown* overthrew held that legally separate Southern black schools were "equal." "In the Jim Crow states that stretched from Delaware to Texas," notes Peter Irons, local school boards in 1930 "spent almost three times as much on each white student as they did on blacks." Racial per-student disparities were especially high in the Deep South states of Alabama (with a white to black per-student spending ratio of 5 to 1), Georgia (4 to 1), Mississippi (6 to 1), and South Carolina (10 to 1). In Clarendon County, South Carolina, site for one of the local cases that were combined in the historic *Brown* law suit, the school board in 1949 spent $179 for each white student, compared to just $43 for each black child. To bring black per-student spending up to the level of whites, Clarendon County would have had to spend an additional half-million dollars on public education.[14]

However, funding differences were only part of a broader inferiority in the quality of education black students received in the South, which was home to 81 percent of the nation's black population prior to World War II. Citing the research of such eminent scholars as Horace Mann Bond, Gunnar Myrdal, and W.E.B. DuBois, the NAACP from the 1930s on found it easy to show that Southern black schools were shockingly substandard in areas that reflected and went beyond fiscal inequity: school buildings, textbooks, teacher qualification, teacher salaries, teacher-student ratios, the number and quality of courses offered, and much more.[15]

During the late 1930s, the American Council of Education dispatched a team of researchers to investigate school conditions in the deep South "Black Belt" from southern Virginian through eastern Texas. "Typical" of such "Negro schools," the Council found, was a black elementary school in Pine Hollow, Alabama:

It is in a dilapidated building, once whitewashed, standing in a rocky field unfit for cultivation. Dust-covered weeds spread a carpet all around, except for an uneven, bare area on one side which looks like a ball field. Behind the school is a small building with a broken, sagging door. As we approach, a nervous, middle-aged woman comes to the door of the school. She greets us in a discouraged voice marked by a speech impediment. Escorted inside, we observe that the broken benches are crowded to three times their normal capacity. Only a few battered books are in sight, and we look in vain for maps or charts. We learn that four grades are assembled here. The weary teacher agrees to permit us to remain while she proceeds with the instruction. She goes to the blackboard and writes an assignment for the first two grades to do while she conducts spelling and word drills for the third and fourth grades. This is the assignment:

"Write your name ten times."

"Draw an dog, an cat, an rat, an boot"

Summarizing its findings, the Council reported that "conditions in and around the rural [black] schools are far from conducive to…the proper personality development of these [black] youth…Poorly prepared instructors, unfit and untrained to cope with rural [black] children and their problems, even under normal circumstances, cannot succeed. These teachers are expected to give the child an appreciation for a cultural heritage about which they themselves are generally unaware. A traditional lifeless curriculum; the harsh, unintelligent disciplinary punishment; and the emphasis on rote learning must share the blame with poverty for the excessive retardation, and for the unrest and dissatisfaction of Negro youth."[16]

Testifying during an earlier phase of the post-WWII Clarendon County litigation that was rolled into the *Brown* case, Howard University Professor Matthew Whitehead noted:[17]

The total value of the buildings, grounds, and furnishings of the two white schools that accommodated 276 children was four times as high as the total for the three Negro schools that accommodated a total of 808 students. The white schools were constructed of brick and stucco; there was one teacher for each 28 children; at the colored schools, there was one teacher for each 47 children. At the white high schools, there was only one class with an enrollment as high as 24; at the Scott's Branch high school for Negroes, classes ranged from 33 to 47. Besides the courses offered at both schools, the curriculum at the white school included biology, typing, and bookkeeping; at the black high school, only agriculture and home economics were offered. There was no running water at one of the two outlying colored grade schools and no electricity at the other one. There were indoor flush toilets at both white schools but no flush toilets, indoors or outdoors, at any of the Negro schools—only outhouses, and not enough of them.

J. Waties Waring, a federal judge in Charleston, South Carolina, was the first justice to hear the NAACP lawsuit on behalf of black students in Clarendon County in 1950. He later recalled "these awful-looking little wooden shacks in the country that were the Negro schools" in the county. "The white schools," he remembered, "were really nothing to be enthusiastic about but they were fairly respectable looking. In the towns, they were generally of brick and some had chimneys, running water, and things of that kind. The Negro schools were just tumbledown dirty shacks with horrible outdoor toilet facilities."[18]

NAACP *Brown* Strategy: From Integration Through Equality to Equality Through Integration

The *Brown* decision, however, said nothing about these harsh inequalities, reflecting a pivotal change in NAACP legal strategy under the leadership of Thurgood Marshall. During the 1930s and 1940s, the NAACP pursued school segregation by launching equal-funding suits against southern boards and universities. By working to equalize teacher salaries, school facilities, textbooks, and the like, the civil rights organization hoped to make "separate but equal" inordinately expensive, thereby indirectly forcing southern authorities to dismantle educational segregation. The idea was to destroy *Plessy v. Ferguson* by insisting on the fulfillment of its never-met promise.

In the case that Marshall took before the Supreme Court in December 1953, however, the NAACP mounted a frontal assault on educational separatism per se, arguing that separate was inherently unequal and unconstitutional: a violation of black children's right to equal protection. Concerns for equity in funding, facilities, and general educational quality were technically omitted as the civil rights lawyers resurrected Charles Sumner's argument that educational race separatism imposed an unjust stigma and inflicted irreparable harm on the self-image of black children. In support of this position, validated by the high court on May 17, 1954, the NAACP famously relied on black psychologist Kenneth Clark's controversial social-psychological "doll studies," which purported to show that, in the words of the *Brown* opinion, "to segregate Negro children from others of similar age and qualifications, solely because of their race, generates a feeling of inferiority as to their status into the community that may affect their hearts and minds in a way unlikely to be undone." That damage to black children's "self-esteem" was taken to inherently translate into unequal educational opportunities for black and white children.[19] Thus, argue many critical black American thinkers today (e.g., Derrick Bell and Roy L. Brooks), did the NAACP send the quest for black educational equality down the path of a fanciful and unrealistic struggle for racial balance in education—a struggle that has diverted blacks from the task of properly and effectively educating their own children, with appropriately equal resources *where they are*: in persistently segregated communities and schools.

No Federal Right to Educational Equity

In subsequent guidelines and rulings promulgated during the 1960s, the federal executive branch and the Supreme Court did make equal teacher qualifications, per-pupil expenditures, extracurricular programs, and physical facilities part of the criteria for determining whether a school district had become properly unitary. In *Milliken v. Bradley II,* a 1977 case following up on the original *Milliken*, the high court ruled that minority inner-city children should receive supplementary educational resources to compensate them for the adverse educational consequence (including the acquisition of "habits of speech, conduct, and attitude reflecting their cultural isolation") of urban segregation when that segregation could be shown to have resulted from enforced racial isolation and discrimination.

These "*Milliken II* remedies" played a prominent role in urban desegregation orders issued after 1977. On the whole, however, the court has emphasized racial mixing rather than minority educational quality and interracial educational equity in determining whether schools have meaningfully met *Brown's* legitimate requirements. According to University of California at Berkeley law professor Rachel Moran, this stress on educational integration over educational quality and equity "set the stage for [*Brown*'s] failure as white flight into the suburbs and the private schools increasingly undercut any hope for meaningful integration."

Faced with the reality of white escape, Moran argues, "The Court might have accorded greater weight to quality education and achievement as alternative to racial balance, thereby preserving *Brown's* viability as an equity initiative." This was most definitely *not* the path taken by the conservative Supreme Court of the post-civil rights era. In *Rodriguez v. San Antonio Independent School District* (1973), civil rights attorneys representing poor children of color attending a poorly funded low-tax school district claimed that Texas' highly inequitable school finance system violated the Equal Protection Clause of the federal constitution. The Court coldly ruled that *equal access to a quality education is not a constitutional right for children in the United States.* The state's regressive public educational finance system, the Court held, was consistent with government's "legitimate state interest" in state and local control of the delivery of educational services. [20]

Meanwhile, the *Milliken II* remedies "evolved," the Harvard Civil Rights Project notes, "not as permanent changes in opportunity structures, but as temporary, supplementary add-ons that are not linked to any systemic effort to redress the harms of segregation." Their "primary function" has been "to serve as a way for school districts and states to sustain a temporary superficial punishment for discrimination."

To make matters worse, the Court refused to establish specific indicators to gauge the effectiveness of the merely temporary remedies in helping minority children overcome the consequences of educational apartheid. The officials of segregated school systems were permitted to stand as judges of the usefulness of their own compensatory programs.

In 1995, the Court reversed a lower federal court's order in Kansas City that had required urban minority students' test scores (taken to be a proxy indication of improved educational equity) to improve before a district could be released from judicial oversight under a federal desegregation order. According to the reactionary Rehnquist Court, the lower court's order could not stand because it did not show precisely how past educational discrimination had generated low achievement for inner-city children. Without such proof, no simple matter to assemble (for reasons that will be touched upon in chapter four of this book), school districts were freed from any requirement to pay for compensatory programs in racially isolated schools.[21]

The struggle for racial educational justice in the post-civil rights era has been sorely challenged, then, by a double legal whammy. The Court's betrayal of *Brown's* integrationist promise has not been accompanied by any reasonable concomitant effort to meet the still-betrayed promise of *Plessy.* As Stan Karp notes, "in the federal courts…de facto segregation doesn't violate the federal constitution" and "unequal funding is [also] not a federal constitutional violation. If you put the two together," Karp asks, "aren't you creating a situation that wouldn't have even satisfied the standards of *Plessy v. Ferguson*?"[22]

SAVAGE INEQUALITIES, UPDATED

The Funding Gap

Predictably, nonwhite students continue to suffer from severe racial school inequities across the nation. According to the Education Trust, in 2001–2003 in twenty states the top quartile of school districts for minority representation received less per-student funding than did the top quartile of districts for nonminority representation. This rather conservative statistic significantly understates the real extent of school funding disparity by race. In Illinois, for example, elementary school per-student funding in 2002–2003 ranged from more than $20,000 in an affluent, 94 percent white Chicago north shore suburb to $7,261 in the 80 percent black and 13 percent Latino south-suburban Chicago suburb of Harvey.

This wide disparity marks a curiously inverted, privilege-preserving relationship between provision and need. The median household income in Lake Forest was $136,142. Just 2 percent of Lake Forest's children lived at or below the poverty level that year. Sixty-one percent of Lake Forest's employed population worked in the U.S. Census Bureau's most elevated employment classification—"management, the professions, or related occupations." In Harvey, where per-student elementary school spending was equivalent to just more than one-third (36 percent) of the per-student pay out in super-affluent, 97 percent white Lake Forest, median household income in 1999 was $31,958 and 28 percent of the children lived in poverty. Only one-fifth of the south suburb's employed population worked in "management, the professions, or related occupations." Similarly, students in the 83 percent black and 11 percent Latino western Chicago suburb of Maywood—home to a 16 percent child poverty rate in 1999—were priced by the school funding system at $6,292 per year, just 31 percent of the annual amount publicly invested in the education of each Lake Forest child.

At the secondary level, north-suburban "Township High School District 113" spent $17,399 per student in 2002–2003. Deerfield, Illinois, home to one of the two high schools in District 113, is 97 percent white. Sixty percent of its employed populace is in the highest occupational category. Its median household income in 1999 was $107,194 and just 2 percent of its children lived in poverty. In the hyper-segregated South Side Chicago neighborhood that hosts the 99.9 percent black Simeon High School, by contrast, 9 percent of the total population lived in what social researchers now call "deep poverty"—at *less than half* of the federal government's notoriously low and inadequate poverty level—and *23 percent* of school-age children were officially poor. In 2002–2003, the Chicago Public Schools spent $6,744 on each Simeon student.

These are just a few examples of a racial school funding gap that reflects and reproduces racial socioeconomic inequity throughout the Chicago area. If you rank the 146 school districts in Chicago's highly segregated Cook County from highest to lowest for per student spending, you find that the top half (seventy-three districts) include just seventeen districts whose students are disproportionately black for the county. The bottom half of districts includes twenty-nine districts that are disproportionately black. Roughly three-fourths (74 percent) of Cook County's black students, a total of more than 221,000, attended the Chicago Public Schools. With a per-student expenditure of $8,786 in 2003, equivalent to less than 45 percent of per-student expenditures in Lake Forest, the central city ranked near the top of the county's bottom half.[23]

Similar funding disparities with strong racial and related city-suburban overtones can be found across the nation. Writing about school inequalities in a book based on his observation of children's lives in New York City's heavily segregated black and Latino South Bronx during the late 1990s, Jonathan Kozol offered the following reflections (which deserve quotation at length) on the extent and meaning of disparity in the allotment of school funding dollars:

> Most disturbing to the teachers who come here to visit from the suburbs are unabated inequalities in public allocation for the education of the children. It's become conventional in social policy debates in recent years to pose what often sound like neutral questions about whether money "really makes much difference" in the education of poor children: questions that are seldom posed when wealthy people contemplate the benefits of sending their own children to expensive private schools or when they move into exclusive suburbs in which public schools are spending more than twice what public schools in the South Bronx are spending on the children in this book. Despite the many ways in which this issue has been clouded, nonetheless, there are few areas in which the value we attribute to a child's life may be so clearly measured as the decisions that we make about the money we believe it's worth investing

in the education of one person's child as opposed to that of someone else's child.

New York City, at the time this book takes place in the late 1990s, spends about $8,000 yearly on each student overall, including special education, but considerably less than this—about $5,000—on each boy or girl in ordinary classrooms of the public elementary schools in the South Bronx...If you had the power to lift up one of these children and plunk him down within one of the relatively wealthy districts of Westchester County, a suburban area that borders New York City to the north, he would suddenly be granted public education worth at least $12,000 every year and he would also have a teacher who is likely to be paid as much as $20,000 more than what a teacher can be paid in the South Bronx. If you could take a slightly longer ride and bring these children to an upper middle class school district such as Great Neck or Manhasset on Long Island, [the South Bronx student] would be in schools where over $18,000 are invested, on the average, in a child's public education every year.

"These are extraordinary inequalities," Kozol adds, "within a metropolitan community that still lays claims to certain vestiges of the humanitarian ideals associated with the age of civil rights and the unforgotten dreams of Dr. Martin Luther King. No matter how these differences may be obscured or understated or complexified by civilized equivocation, they do tell us something about how we value [inner-city children of color] as human beings, both in their present status as small children and in their future destinies as adult citizens." [24]

Three years after these painful and poignant paragraphs were published and even after the New York City-based Campaign for Fiscal Equity won a state-level lawsuit calling for increased funding to guarantee "a sound basic education" for children in New York City's public schools, per-pupil spending in the city ($10,500 on average) was still less than half of per-student expenditures in Manhasset. As this chapter was being written in the winter of 2004, a three-referee panel appointed by the New York State Supreme Court determined that it will cost an additional $15 billion for New York City's 1.1 million disproportionately black and Latino students to receive an "adequate" education, while students in affluent white districts on Long Island and north of the City attend public schools funded on par with elite private academies.[25]

What School Money Buys

The higher priced children of Manhasset, Lake Forest, Highland Park, Illinois, Grosse Point and Livonia, Michigan (outside Detroit), Shorewood, Wisconsin (north of Milwaukee), or Mission Hill (outside Kansas City, Missouri) enjoy numerous advantages purchased with relatively generous educational funding allotments. These extra school rewards of birth and residence include significantly smaller student-to-teacher ratios, something that is generally understood to enhance learning opportunities. These areas also offer considerably higher teacher salaries that tend to draw skilled and dedicated instructors away from less well-funded inner-city and rural school districts (a staple piece of urban-educational folklore relates the story of the passionate and effective ghetto teacher who finally breaks down and takes a less hectic and better-compensated position in an affluent white suburb). Then there are the "dozens of [money-] associated matters such as the provision of attractive libraries, good exercise facilities, intensive counseling and guidance in selection of a course of study that will lead to university admission." These and "other offerings, both pedagogic and aesthetic," convey what Kozol calls "a sense of democratic amplitude" and "shape an ambience of opportunity and graciousness in day-to-day existence."[26]

In a comparison that has its rendition in every U.S. metropolitan area, Harvard education professor Pedro Noguera paints a revealing Bay Area contrast between the predominantly white and middle-class Willard Middle School in Berkeley, California and the predominantly black Lowell Middle School in impoverished west Oakland:[27]

> While the hallways [in Lowell] are dark and dank, the hallways [in Willard] are bright with natural illumination from skylights in the ceilings, and grass and trees over the campus. While Lowell is enclosed by a fence approximately 15 feet high that borders the perimeters of the campus, Willard and its facilities—pool, playing field, tennis and basketball courts—are accessible to its neighborhood and the general public. The design of the two schools suggests that whereas Lowell regards its community with suspicion and fear, Willard perceives the community as an ally and its facilities are regarded by residents as a public resource and asset. In fact, a beautiful garden in front of Willard was created and maintained by the school's neighbors.

Education as an Unaffordable Luxury in an Original *Brown* County

There is little feeling of "democratic amplitude" and "graciousness" in the schools of Clarendon County, site for one of the historic *Brown* lawsuits. According to Ellis Cose, the county's predominantly black rural schools continue to be victimized my massive funding inequalities and related facility disparities. "Were it not for the American flags proudly flying over the roofs," Cose noted in 2004, these schools "*might have been plucked out of some impoverished country that sees education as a luxury it can barely afford* [emphasis added]."²⁸ Further:

> Take a tour of Jasper County and you will find a middle school with a drainpipe in the corridor, which occasionally spills sewage into the hallway. You'll find labs were the equipment doesn't work, so that children have to simulate, rather perform, experiments. You'll see walls ruined by mould and moisture and buildings where "the infrastructure is so poorly done our computer systems are down more than they are up." In nearby Clarendon County, conditions are not much better. Were Thurgood Marshall to find himself in Clarendon County today, "he would think *[Brown]* had been reversed," state Senator John Marshall told a visitor in December 2003. "There are a couple of nice buildings, but you get outside and there're no decent playgrounds. You're talking about teachers who are limited to five sheets of paper a day for mimeograph work. You're dealing with books that are 10 years behind the times," or, worse, simply not to be had.

The only white children in these poor, inferior southern and segregated schools come from families that cannot afford to send their children to the private schools (once termed "segregation academies") that sprang up across the South when public school desegregation was enforced. Jasper County superintendent William Singleton told Cose that the expansion of such private white schools "continued with a dual system" that has led to "a steady decline of the [public] educational system in Jasper County." The white "folks in power" in rural South Carolina see no point, Cose learned, in giving predominantly black districts the money they need to offer their children a quality education. "Singleton," Cose notes, "would love to be able to hire teachers from nearby Beaufort (home to Hilton Head's array of fancy eateries and resorts), but notes that Beaufort can pay $2,500 to $8,000 more."[29]

"We Didn't Know How Screwed We Were Getting"

In his recent book *Final Test: The Battle For Adequacy in America's Schools*, veteran education writer Peter Schrag tells the story of a group of minority San Francisco high school students who became plaintiffs in an ACLU lawsuit seeking increased school funding from the state of California in 2001. The students' complaints, Schrag noted, were "common enough" in nonwhite urban schools:

> There, as is often the case in schools that service poor students, not enough textbooks—because there was often only one set per teacher for several classes, no one could take a book home—and so teachers struggled to copy enough pages to hand out to their classes...There were the strings of substitute teachers. There were the dirty and often inaccessible bathrooms, [including]...ones that, when they were open, had "that smell, that horrible smell"...There were labs without equipment and classrooms where...there weren't enough seats or desks...These classrooms were too hot in the fall and spring, especially on the sunny side of the building, and too cold in the winter...There were the mouse droppings...and the bird "doodoo" in the gym, where the birds had come in through broken windows...There was the class called Modern World where the teacher got sick in the fall 'and we just had a bunch of substitutes instead...There was the constant turnover of teachers.

These problems reflected what Schrag called "situations that are so familiar that they're hardly noticed anymore except by the people who are stuck in [poor minority] schools: falling ceiling tiles, leaking roofs, insufficient lighting, cafeterias and hallways converted to classrooms, filthy and nonfunctional toilets, windows that don't open or shut, buildings where teachers and children freeze in the winter and swelter in the spring and fall, and, where schools run year-round , as they do in many urban districts, in the summer as well." Such problems, which routinely plague poor and nonwhite schools, can be found, Schrag notes, "anywhere you look—in New York City, in Los Angeles, in rural Alabama or North Carolina, in Philadelphia, in Chicago."[30]

Regarding North Carolina, Schrag learned, one critical race disparity has to do with differential access to calculators. In that state, where high school students are expected to employ graphing calculators on standardized state tests, "teachers in poor schools have to borrow them on test days from other schools and let students try to use the calculators on the tests without enough practice. In some districts, parents are required to buy them for their children out of their pockets. The same is often true for team, band, and cheerleader uniforms." [31]

Students, teachers, and staff from the schools that gave rise to the California suit told Schrag about the shortage of advanced placement classes and of basic courses required for college. Schrag learned about school laboratories that "lack[ed] enough materials to do more than one or two experiments a year" and students who "spent whole [class] period[s] reading or copying notes from an overhead projector because the books can't go home." At San Francisco's predominantly minority Balboa High School (one-fourth black, one-fourth Latino, one-fourth Filipino, 4 percent white, and the remainder Chinese or Samoan), the average class had thirty-four to thirty-five students.

Balboa's student-plaintiffs were shocked and outraged when one of their social-studies teachers took them on a series of school exchange visits. Those visits included a weekend retreat to Marin Academy, "an expensive private school just north of San Francisco, where the tuition is $21,000 a year, plus books and other various fees." Visiting Marin was a, well, educational experience for Balboa's students. It taught them "what things were like on the other side of the tracks." "The really good about the Marin exchange," one Balboa student reported, "was that we didn't know how screwed we were getting; now we understood." In the elite academy, they were amazed to learn, the average class size was fifteen. "For its 385 students," Schrag notes, Marin had "*nearly as many teachers, forty-nine, as Balboa had for its 1,200.*" [emphasis added][32]

The students of Balboa would understand the complaints of Mary Johnson, head of a parent advocacy group seeking to improve educational quality in highly impoverished minority neighborhoods in and around Los Angeles. In the highly impoverished black and Latino Los Angeles inner-ring suburb of South Gate, Johnson wrote in 2004:[33]

Most of the parents work in service industry or perform physical labor for [the] minimum wage and most have no formal education. Every morning you see adults walk to the bus stop to catch the bus to work as maids and car washers in cities where they can't afford to live. Folks from my community clean expensive hotels where we can't afford to stay and wash cars that we can't afford to buy. The majority of our parents complain of lower back pain because of the physical labor of bending and lifting. We work hard to make a better life for our children. The outside world classifies our community as a ghetto, but we call it home.

In our neighborhood, you will see advertisements for liquor stores, but never a child reading a book. There are also advertisement posters from big sporting companies programming our children to believe that the only way out of our neighborhood is through sports. The first gifts we buy our boys are footballs or basketballs because in our hearts we feel that our earnings won't allow us the opportunity to send our children to college. Society has forced parents of color to send our children the wrong messages. There isn't one bookstore within a 15 miles radius. In the local schools there are no book clubs on the school campus.

Part of the problem, Johnson argued, is that South Gate's schools and teachers are inadequately equipped and—to introduce a problem to which I shall return throughout this book—too authoritarian to nurture an appropriately critical, democratic, and oppositional sense of resistance to the dominant anti-intellectual messages of the corporate mass culture:

There are many barriers that parents of color must overcome. In many schools, children aren't being taught to be critical thinkers, *so they aren't able to challenge the conditions they face* [emphasis added]. This is one of the main reasons that our children do badly in college. College success is based on critical thinking. Critical thinking ensures that our children will be better prepared for a higher level of learning. However, when students of color display critical thinking, they are looked at as being disrespectful. When our children challenge a teacher in the classroom about educational issues, they often are sent to the Dean's office for disrupting the class.

To be critical thinkers students must have access to learning materials. It seems that our State and Federal governments give monies to local school districts, but ask for no accountability for the use of that money. State laws require that every child has a book for each subject matter. In our neighborhood we get copies or dittoes of books. Books are needed for homework and for test preparation. Children in affluent schools and communities have two sets of books, one for the classroom and one set for home. Many children of color work with books that are outdated or with pages missing. Many school districts have failed to purchase books and materials. It seems year after year there are fewer books than in previous years.

Many young teachers lack experience and depend heavily on books as a reference for teaching. There are a high percentage of un-credentialed teachers in our neighborhoods as compared to affluent neighborhoods. Many teachers are teaching out of their subject matter. Some children have a different substitute-teacher every day.... The environment that our children go to schools in is second-class. Our children are forced to go to schools where the classrooms are overcrowded. Most classroom ratios are forty students to one teacher and no aide. There are not enough open bathrooms. There is also a lack of toilet paper and hygiene products. Some of the schools we visit have lead poison in the water, exposed chips of lead paint, rusted pipes, water damaged ceilings, and holes in the walls of the restrooms. Some classrooms have no heat or air conditioning.

Digital Division

Balboa's students and Mary Johnson and the teachers and students of the South Bronx and Chicago's South Side would be intrigued, no doubt, to learn that all seventh- and eighth-graders in the relatively affluent, predominantly white town of Freeport, Maine receive their own free laptop computers from their local public school.[34]

Speaking of computers, one small but relevant way to gauge educational race disparity in the post-*Brown* era is to compare high school Web sites. Go to the site of a predominantly white, affluent high school and chances are that you will be favorably impressed. The site will likely be pleasingly and professionally constructed, exhibiting a rich content including a large number of school photographs and a plethora of achievement-related information, including links and advice on application and admission to good universities and colleges. Find, if you can, the Web site of a poor and predominantly black and/or Latino high school for comparison and you will, in all likelihood, get some new "virtual" appreciation of racial school inequalities. Chicago's South Side Simeon High School's Web site, as of December 2004, is typical for poor and segregated high schools. It includes little more than a few lines giving the name, the address of the school, its sports teams' name, the name of its principal, and the year Simeon was constructed.

The Lankford Curve

As previously suggested, in the United States poorer, browner, and blacker students tend to be instructed not only by quantitatively fewer teachers (per student) but also, on average, by qualitatively inferior teachers. According to a detailed analysis published by the *Chicago Sun Times*, fully 19 percent of the teachers in Chicago's heavily black and Latino public schools failed at least one basic skills subject matter test in 2001. The percentage of public school teachers who failed one such test was five times higher in the central city than in the Chicago suburbs. Over 85 percent of Illinois' "worst teachers" (as measured by skills tests) were located in Chicago, home to just 18 percent of the state's teachers.

These findings were consistent with research by economist Hamilton Lankford. Lankford has found an almost perfect correlation—what educational researchers now call "the Lankford Curve"—between low-teacher training, low-measured teacher ability, and high-student poverty in schools—a correlation found to hold relevance within big-city school districts as well as between city and suburban districts.[35]

This disturbing correlation and the broader school inequality of which it is a part is especially unfortunate in an economic period in which educational achievement plays a greater role than ever before in determining labor market and socioeconomic outcomes. As Jeffrey Henig notes:[36]

> While many schools are delivering a mediocre product that sells their students short, for some children, especially those living in large central cities with high minority populations and heavy concentrations of the poor, the tale is much more tragic. Broad economic changes are putting a higher and higher premium on educational attainment, yet these students languish in decrepit school buildings, where many of the teachers lack the skills and training they should have, the resources to meet their special challenges, and/or the enthusiasm and faith that might once have led to consider education their mission and not simply their job.

Militarized Schooling and Zero Tolerance

The teacher quality gap is strongly related to critical moral, pedagogical, and curricular gaps between white and minority schools. On top of the material and aesthetic disadvantages discussed so far, racially isolated urban minority students' struggle to create successful and democratic lives is all-too-often challenged by teachers, school officials, city leaders, and a broader mainstream culture that tend to see them as inherently dangerous, violent, irresponsible, lazy, selfish, anti-achievement, and generally incapable or unworthy of elevated thoughts, higher education, useful work and good citizenship. One expression of this harsh, racially tinged judgment is what Henry Giroux and Susan Searls Giroux call "the militarization of [urban-minority] schools—now complete with security guards, drug-sniffing dogs, see-through knapsacks, metal detectors, and zero-tolerance policies that threaten those who misbehave not only with expulsion but with actual jail time."[37] By Pedro Noguera's observation, many inner-city schools have been victimized by an expensive and practically militarist obsession "security." "Some [such] schools," Noguera notes, "have been transformed into fortress-like facilities, fully equipped with metal detectors, surveillance cameras, security guards, and police officers." Poor districts make expensive investments in such quasi-militarist school staff and technology even while they dismantle academic programs to meet budget shortfalls.

Ironically, Noguera observes, schools that "rely on guards and metal detectors rarely feel like safe places." When teachers are "removed from the disciplinary process and replaced by guards," Noguera finds, "safety and order may actually decrease." A former member of Oakland, California's School Board, Noguera first became concerned about urban schools' security emphasis while visiting a high school in west Oakland during the early 1990s. "I asked the security guard who escorted me how they managed to keep the walls free of graffiti. The guard laughed and responded, '*This is a lock-down facility.*'" [emphasis added][38]

Even in less security-obsessed racially mixed schools, it is worth noting, the disciplinary, punishment-centered approach seems to be especially geared toward children of color. In one high school that was 38 percent white and 38 percent black in 1998, blacks comprised 70 percent of all off-campus suspensions.[39] In an integrated elementary school that his daughter attended, to give another example, the black law professor Roy L. Brooks noted in 1996, "A special room was set-aside for mis-behaving students. It was called the Discipline Room, and the name was written across the door. Students could walk by and see who was in it; most of the time most of the children were black…The principal confided in me that it anguishes her to peer into the room each morning only to see a sea of little black faces. Too many white teachers," Brooks observed, "harbor negative attitudes and perceptions about African-American students. Some of these teachers prefer not to teach them; oth-ers simply do not like them as individuals."[40]

Skill, Drill, Grill, and Mind-Kill

In another, related expression of the post-*Brown*-era's negative ruling on hyper-segregated black and Latino children's capa-bilities and character, those children are heavily targeted by the soulless, mind-numbing, and authoritarian standardized-test-based curriculum that public authorities impose with special vengeance on the urban poor. Teachers in predominantly black inner-city schools routinely report experiencing inordinate pressure from school authorities to gear instruction toward the standardized achievement tests that determine which schools are honored as successful and which are shamed as failures, and sanctioned—often with severe budgetary consequences—and sometimes even closed. Under this top-down high-stakes test-ing regime, classroom experience becomes dull and unimagi-native, privileging the authoritarian, mind-narrowing search for the right answer over the democratic and mind-opening pursuit of the good question.

Test-targeted curriculum emphasizes rote, quasi-vocation-al "skill and drill" classroom methods over critical thinking and the cultivation of intelligent and active citizenship among students. It should be understood as a form of authoritarian, political and moral de-skilling. As Kozol notes, it subordinates "critical consciousness" to "the goal of turning minority children into examination soldiers—unquestioning and docile followers of proto-military regulations."[41] Under its reign, Henry Giroux notes:[42]

> Teachers are prevented from taking risks and designing their own lessons as the pressure to achieve passing test scores produces highly scripted and regimented forms of teaching. In this context, worksheets become a substitute for critical teaching and rote memorization takes the place of in-depth thinking. Behaviorism becomes the preferred model of pedagogy and substitutes a mind-numbing emphasis on methods that are critical, moral, and political in substance. Learning facts and skills in reading and math becomes more important than genuine understanding. Academic success therefore becomes largely a measure of one's speed in taking high-stakes standardized tests, rather than the ability to engage knowledge with thoughtfulness and critical analytical skills.

The great Brazilian radical educator and pedagogy theorist Paulo Freire would certainly have recognized the current test-based curriculum that is so ubiquitously present in the nation's deeply shamed poor and racially isolated schools as a version what he described as "the 'banking' concept of education, in which the scope of action allowed to the students extends only so far as receiving, filing, and storing the deposits. They do, it is true, have the opportunity to become collectors or cataloguers of the things they store. But in the last analysis, it is the people themselves are filed away through the lack of creativity, transformation, and knowledge in this (at least) misguided system."[43] Under this "banking" pedagogy, whereby students are turned into passive recipients of strictly limited information poured in by supposedly all-knowing instructors, students are rendered unable, in Mary Johnson's words "to challenge" the oppressive "conditions they face"—conditions that have as much to do with life outside as well as within school halls.

It is intriguing in this context to learn that the former head of the Chicago Public Schools, the Caucasian Paul Vallas, claimed that he was inspired to make test-based pedagogy the model for his city's majority black schools by reading National Guard training manuals for soldiers.[44] It is interesting also to learn that, as Asa Hillard, III notes, "today's scripted, cookie-cutter, minimum-competency managed instruction, sometimes [managed] by private contractors, with severely reduced parent and community involvement, is offered mainly in low-income minority cultural group schools. Affluent public or private schools," Hillard, III observes, "rarely if ever use the scripted, non-intellectual programs. This is the new segregation."[45]

Some contemporary school "equity" activists prefer to ignore this "new segregation." They prefer to mute any qualms they or others might have about "drill and grill" teaching in their quest to use test-score "achievement gap" data to make the case for the provision of more adequate school funding dollars to poor and segregated schools.[46]

Beyond its deadening impact on children's passion and capacity for critical thinking and deeply engaged learning, the "drill and grill" testing regime drives many of the best current and potential teachers away from urban schools. It tends to undermine the professional enthusiasm of those who, as Jeffrey Henig says, consider education "their mission and not simply their job." Those teachers prefer settings more conducive to the well-rounded practice of the pedagogical craft, where students and parents would never tolerate the "teacher-proof," test-obsessed curriculum that too commonly predominates in inner-city schools.

"Dead Weight": High-Stakes Testing as Incentive
to Push Black Students Out of School and into Prison

Another problem with the high-stakes testing regime relates to the nation's hidden black and Latino high school graduation crisis. "Just at the time when our schools should be making every effort to educate Hispanic and African-American children and keep them in school," notes Chicago school reform expert Don Moore, "high stakes standardized tests (which are being used to judge whether schools are 'failing') create a powerful incentive to actually *push* students out of school." In "a misguided effort to raise test scores in the easiest possible way," Moore notes, "some [Chicago schools] are choosing to *push out low-scoring students rather than to educate these students.*" Moore relates the chilling story of "the assistant principal of one inner-city Chicago high school [who] told the press, 'the school is penalized for these kids. We want quality more than quantity. *If that means removing dead weight, we will remove dead weight.*" One frequent practice in Chicago high schools is to drop students from the school's roster for poor attendance and then refuse their request to be reenrolled.[47] According to a 2004 Harvard Civil Rights Project study, "a number of recent Chicago 'dropouts' report that they were pushed out of public high schools by officials who told them that their truancy or bad grades showed that they did want to be there." Illinois law, this study goes on to note, "allows school officials to 'disenroll' 16-year-olds "who can't be expected to graduate by their 21st birthday." Expulsion is a marvelous test-score booster for inner-city schools, a factor behind the fact that the number of students expelled by Chicago's public schools has "skyrocketed" since the mid-1990s, with black students being banished from classrooms at a rate three times higher than whites and Hispanics.[48] Such policies and practices are widespread in minority city schools and play no small part in creating the shockingly low national four-year graduation rates of black (50.2 percent) and Latino (53.2 percent) high school students.[49]

According to one recent academic estimate, it is worth noting that half of the nation's black male high-school dropouts will be incarcerated—moving, often enough, from quasi-carceral lock-down high schools to the real "lock down" thing—at some point in their lives. These dropouts are over-represented among the one in three African American males aged sixteen- to twenty-years-old who are under one form of supervision by the U.S. criminal justice system: parole, probation, jail, or prison.[50]

Tracking: "Secret Apartheid"

Important issues of pedagogical style and content aside, public school systems tend to steer minority children away from high school courses meant to prepare children for higher education. Black high school students are under-represented in such classes—algebra, geometry, calculus, laboratory science, foreign languages, and advanced placement humanities and social science courses. They are over-represented in more "vocationally" focused remedial "general track" classes where math equals common sense arithmetic and science is never concretely learned through experimental, hands-on procedures. Even in "racially mixed schools," Steinhorn and Diggs-Brown note, "honors and accelerated classes tend to be mostly white, and special-education, basic-skills, and vocational classes tend to be mostly black."[51] Such race-tracking, which "raised discrimination to an art form" in Rockford, Illinois (according to a federal judge), is commonly considered to be an unavoidable practice for urban school systems who wish to prevent white flight from racially mixed schools and/or to minimize white opposition to the entrance of black students to predominantly white schools. "School districts," one academic study noted in the late 1990s, "have been willing to trade-off black access to equal educational opportunities for continued white enrollment in the school system."[52]

By Kozol's observation during the late 1990s, some of the South Bronx's disadvantaged black and Latino parents were quite familiar with—and resentful of—the deep injustice at the heart of curricular regimes that seek to mold poor and minority youth for low-level clerical, industrial, service, and sales positions while preparing affluent white youth for the upper reaches of the occupational and income pyramid:

> Many people in [the South Bronx neighborhood] Mott Haven do a lot of work to make sure they are well informed about conditions in their children's public schools. Some also know a great deal more about the schools that serve the children of privileged than many of the privileged themselves may recognize. They know that "business math" is not the same as calculus and that "job-readiness instruction" is not European history or English literature. They know that children of rich people do not often spend semesters of their teenage years in classes where they learn to type an application for an entry-level clerical position; they know these wealthy children are too busy learning composition skills and polishing their French pronunciation and received preparation for the SATs. They come to understand the process by which a texture of entitlement is stitched together for some children while it is denied to others. They also understand that, as the years go by, some of these children will appear to have deserved one kind of role in life, and some another.

Just a few years before Kozol was gathering the stories and data that led to these eloquent observations, the New York City chapter of the national social justice advocacy group ACORN sent white, Latino, and black parents on test visits to sixteen different New York city school districts to examine racial and ethnic disparities in parents' ability to become involved in the provision of quality educational opportunities to their children. The testers posed as parents seeking information relevant to the possible enrollment of their children in each school visited. In a study bearing the title *Secret Apartheid*, ACORN discovered that:

> Black and Latino parents were permitted to speak with an educator less than half as often as white parents. White parents were given tours of schools two and a half times more often than black and Latino parents. White parents often received "A" list treatment while people of color were relegated to the "B" list. Access to information about gifted programs appeared to vary by the race of the parent making the inquiry...in 32 visits to [gifted New York City] schools, African-American and Latino testers succeeded in speaking with an educator (principal, teacher, etc,) only four times. Only one of the four was a principal. In five visits, black or Hispanic testers were prevented from getting information from various school offices by security guards who refused them entry to the school; a white tester also encountered this problem.

ACORN also found and documented the systematic under-availability in poor and minority Middle Schools of courses likely to improve performance on the standardized tests that determine eligibility for the city's superior "magnet" high schools.[53]

A "TOTAL STRUCTURE" OF INEQUALITY

Whence these persistently savage and highly racialized school inequalities? School funding and equity activists are right to place special blame on the American system's distinctive heavy, privilege-preserving dependence on local property taxes to fund public education.[54] Since local property wealth differs widely across school districts, such reliance naturally translates into significant discrepancies in the resources available for local communities to invest in schools.

In the Chicago area during the late 1990s, local property-based tax capacity ranged from $107 per household in the poor black south-suburban town of Robbins to $6,954 per household in the affluent and predominantly white west-suburban town of Oak Brook,[55] home to a large number of corporate office buildings and upper-end retail outlets. The tax base available for education in Lake Forest was thirty-eight times higher than the comparable base in black, south-suburban Harvey, Illinois.

Beyond providing more total resources per student in rich districts, these tax-base disparities ironically mean that homeowners in places like Harvey and Robbins are taxed at higher rates than their affluent white counterparts to maintain grossly inferior educational institutions. In 2000, the Chicago area's twenty most well-funded school districts taxed themselves at just $1.64 per $1,000 of assessed value to pay for their superior schools. The twenty least well-funded districts (including Harvey) had to pay nearly $5 per $100 of assessed value to sustain their much more poorly funded schools. Under the regressive U.S. school financing system, the Education Trust notes, "a local district fortunate enough to have high value commercial real estate in its tax base can provide abundant funding for its schools with a relatively low tax rate; a district without that wealth is stuck with a terrible dilemma—impose inordinately high tax rates that burden homeowners and defer the kind of business development they need, or provide substandard funding in their schools."[56]

As my Chicago-area examples suggest, this local tax disparity is related to differences of skin color. In a nation with more than 16,000 separate and unequal school districts, where property is becoming more and more unequal than ever, where black median household net worth ($8,000 in 1999) is equivalent to less than one-tenth of white median household net worth ($81,450) and communities remain strongly segregated by race, reliance on local property wealth to pay for schools "functions," Stan Karp notes, "as a sorting mechanism for class and race privilege," permitting "pockets of 'elite schooling' to exist within the public system."[57]

To be sure, local property tax reliance does not inherently translate into racial school funding inequity. It is because housing markets and thus communities are still harshly segregated by race that this inherently class-stratified funding method also reproduces racial inequality. At the same time, many of the core educational inequalities between white and minority students and schools cannot simply be reduced to school funding disparities. These include the low socioeconomic status and numerous related difficulty "extra-school" circumstances that a disproportionately large number of black children experience as a result of broad societal race and class apartheid, reflecting conditions and consequences that will provide the main subject matter for the fourth chapter of this book. One critical disparity that especially resists reduction to funding inequality is what Kozol calls "the insidious acceptance of apartheid pedagogies"—the "drill and grill" classroom instruction and assessment methods that "leave no room for the more wholesome and authentic forms of learning that cannot be measured by empirical assessments"—as "the favored instruments for teaching apartheid's children."[58]

Kozol's formulation is a reminder that segregation is more then just separation, legal or otherwise. Classic southern segregation, Asa Hillard, III notes, "was a total system of domination, which included the uses of all major societal institutions—law, mass media, criminal justice, religion, science, school curriculum, spectator sports, and music, etc.… 'Integrating the schools,'" Hillard notes, "did not eliminate the ideology of white supremacy from which 'segregation' derived."[59]

The "new segregation" and current white supremacy is also a "total" and many-sided system within and beyond schools. It includes a segregated curriculum, racially disparate disciplinary approaches, and numerous other "savage inequalities"—not the least of which are divergent teacher opinions on student capabilities and character that persist even where inner-city per-student spending approaches suburban levels and in the nation's all-too-rare well-integrated schools.

On that cautionary note, the next chapter turns to some of the accomplishments and limits of the recent state-level struggle for educational fiscal equity between and among segregated schools in the post-*Brown* era.

3

SEPARATE BUT ADEQUATE

Laws for the liberal education of youth, especially for the lower classes of people, are so extremely wise and useful that to a humane and generous mind, no expense for this purpose be thought extravagant.

—John Adams, 1776[1]

No parent or student should have to offer scientific proof that attractive schools with working toilets and decent classroom environments are more productive than those without. None should be asked how they knew that having rats in their classrooms impaired their ability to learn. Nor should any school have to justify good libraries and after-school programs in art or music with test scores and college attendance rates. What's perfectly clear is that when people can afford it, they opt for the schools with rich resources, and often struggle (and sometimes lie and cheat) to get their children into the right schools.

—Peter Schrag, 2003[2]

By the early 1970s, many educational justice advocates inspired by *Brown's* declared promise of educational equality had decided to focus on the neo-*Plessy*-ite issue of "fiscal equity" between racially separate schools. "Given the difficulty of integrating black and white students with their seemingly fleeing white counterparts," Derrick Bell notes, a growing number of civil rights activists "decided that...we should concentrate on desegregating the money."[3] These activists knew that children of color were disproportionately represented among those who attended under-funded schools and schools districts, particularly in the central city areas the *Milliken* decision encouraged white families to abandon. As advocates turned their attention to "fiscal equity," they looked to the states, for the Supreme Court ruled (in 1973, as we have seen,) that American children enjoyed no federal constitutional right to an education, much less to an equal education. Relying on state-level equal protection clauses and, more commonly by the 1990s, on state constitutional "education clauses" that made quality schooling a basic right, educational justice proponents turned to state courts and legislatures.

They have done so with no small success. State courts in at least twenty of forty states where school funding equity lawsuits have been initiated since 1971 have ordered state governments to dismantle school finance systems that have been deemed to violate the principles of fairness and adequacy. In the first such state-level victory for equity activists, *Serrano v. Priest*, the California Supreme Court ordered California to embrace a philosophy of "fair taxation." Wealthy districts were required to share resources with poor districts to promote literal per-student funding equity across districts.[4]

Thirty-two years later, to mention the most recent high-profile state-level victory for the fiscal equity movement, the New York State Supreme Court ordered that that state's high reliance on local property taxes to finance schools had unconstitutionally cheated the public school students of New York City. Those students, the court held, were being denied their state-constitutional right to receive "a sound basic education." The court gave the state's governor four hundred days to determine the real cost of a "sound basic education" and to devise ways to make sure that all school districts could meet that cost. In November 2004, a court-appointed panel determined that the state would have to pay $15 billion to help New York City's public school students receive the level of schooling to which they are entitled—a victory for the New York City-based Campaign for Fiscal Equity (CFE).[5]

Similarly, on January 3, 2005, the Kansas Supreme Court ruled in *Montoy v. State* that the Kansas legislature had failed to meet its constitutional requirement "to make suitable provision for finance of the public schools." The Kansas legislature was given until April 12, 2005 to improve its funding system so that all students, not just the residents of property-rich districts, can attend schools sufficiently funded to meet "the actual and shifting costs of providing 'intellectual, educational, vocational and scientific improvement,' as mandated by the state constitution."[6]

Such state-level rulings and the campaigns that press for them and for subsequent legislative actions to adjust school financing upward for poor schools are certainly welcome and likely to be encouraged by anyone who supports *Brown*'s dream of educational quality for children of color. At the same time, it is should be noted that litigants and courts fighting and ruling on fiscal equity rarely make any explicit reference to specifically racial disparity in local and state school funding systems. Beyond that interesting deletion, moreover, the effectiveness of state-level lawsuits as a strategy for delivering real educational justice to "Jim Crow's children" is qualified in ten key ways.

First, a federalist state-by-state strategy tends to lose sight of critical federal funding issues. As Stan Karp noted in the fall of 2003, more than five months into the illegal U.S. invasion of Iraq, making "good on the promise of educational equity and excellence will take tens of billions of dollars over many years, the kinds of sums that have been poured into the military for decades" The $87 billion that the White House requested for the next year of the Iraq occupation war, Karp observed, "would pay the salaries of more than 1.6 million new elementary school teachers. It [was] also *equal to the combined budget deficits in all the states for fiscal 2003–2004.*" [emphasis added] This as federal investigations "documented a need for more than $110 billion in construction and renovation of K–12 facilities" and federal funding of local schools "dropped to their lowest post-WWII levels in the 1980s and had risen only slightly since."[7]

Second, a state-level strategy leaves the struggle for quality education at the mercy of very jurisdictionally divergent political, legal, constitutional, and judicial alignments. In New Jersey, the state Supreme Court's famous (among equity advocates) 1990 *Abbott II* decision quickly became "the gold standard" for equity supporters by defining equity for poor children as actual equivalency with per-student spending in the state's one hundred richest districts and ordering rapid supplemental spending to meets the additional special needs of poor children. Right next door, in New York, a jurisdiction with historically higher race and class funding disparities, activists were unable to win an equity lawsuit until fifteen years later and the state's high court rejected egalitarian sentiments. It ruled that that poor children were entitled only to "a sound basic education" and left it up to the state legislature to determine the precise meaning of that highly and almost endlessly contested term through "an extended political (and perhaps legal) struggle in the midst of perpetual budget crisis."[8]

Third, it should be acknowledged that the pursuit of true school fiscal equity in a context of broad racial and class hierarchy and related racial segregation is somewhat chimerical.

Parents in rich white districts are free to supplement public school funding, however configured, with ample private contributions through PTA fundraisers, corporate contributions, and the like. Affluent parents remain free, of course, to send their children to expensive private schools that do not have to report their certainly high per-student spending rates.

Fourth, there are strong reasons to doubt that even fully equalized funding that is accompanied by significant additional money for inner-city schools can make the dramatic improvements in test-measured student achievement that equity advocates commonly tout as the promised outcome of increased public expenditure for poor schools. As Bell notes, "schools in poor, segregated neighborhoods that have been marginalized for decades will not suddenly achieve high quality education and produce students competitive with those of traditionally privileged schools just because they are given equal funding. That is like expecting a Pinto to keep up with a Porsche simply because their engines both run gasoline. Remediation for present-day inequalities cannot alone compensate for ancient injuries."[9] We might add that "remediation" for savage school-specific inequalities cannot to make up for the educational inequalities that are rooted in extra-school factors of broad societal class and race apartheid: poverty, unemployment, family disintegration, endemic community violence and substance abuse, and so on. Many experts, as we shall see in the next chapter, think that these nonschool factors are the biggest obstacles to effective schooling for minority children and the largest cause of the much-bemoaned minority student standardized-test achievement-gap.

Fifth, it is much easier to get court orders striking down state funding programs than it is to get state governments to set up new systems that provide equity. Activists have pursued a number of strategies to reduce states' inherently unequal reliance on local property taxes: the redistribution of some property tax revenues from rich to poor districts; the replacement of property taxes with other, generally sales, taxes; the redefinition of state funding formulas so that more funds are directed to poor districts. But "no particular financial mechanism," Karp notes, "guarantees either equity or quality in education" or ensures that "adequate funds will be available." A number of states have introduced promising new formulas pledging more school funding only "to cut and modify them once the higher costs become clear. If the [state government's] controlling motivation is desire to cut property taxes and hold down educational spending rather than promote quality or equity," Karp observes, "it may not matter what fiscal mechanism is chosen" to advance funding reform. This limit is especially relevant and critical today in a context of rampant and interrelated state and federal fiscal crisis created by economic slowdown, hyper-regressive tax cuts, and the ascendancy of neoliberal and neoconservative ideologies that justify the starvation of key public programs and de-legitimize the struggle for social justice and equality.[10]

California, site of the first state-court school funding equity victory, provides an early and cautionary example of the political difficulties involved. After the California Supreme Court clarified and specified its mandate in a second *Serrano* decision in 1976, that state's legislature adopted a system that centralized state property taxes and redistributed the resulting dollars to equalize funding across districts. One year later, affluent white California activists and voters reacted to this egalitarian reform by passing "Proposition 13," a popular initiative that significantly cut and capped property taxes. "As a result," notes University of California-Berkeley law professor Rachel Moran, California "school funding dropped dramatically and California's vaunted public educational system plummeted from the top ten to the bottom ten in per-pupil expenditures." Moran thinks that this sorry episode is "a sober reminder of de Tocqueville's warning that the price of equality in a democratic society can be mediocrity."[11] It is more accurate to see the California story as a reminder that socioeconomic inequality undercuts democracy, enabling those with differentially high wealth to disproportionately influence policy to preserve and deepen privilege.

During the early 1990s, to give a more recent example, the Kentucky legislature moved quickly in accord with a state court order to considerably increase its investment in basic educational adequacy for poor children. The state increased its yearly minimum public school spending dramatically, from $2,898 in 1992 to $7,072 in 2003. Fourteen years after this "landmark" funding reform (heralded for inspiring equity efforts across the nation), however, the vast majority of Kentucky school districts sued the state for failing to put sufficient money into education. According to a front-page story in the *New York Times* in December 2004, these districts "argue that that the state's financial formulas have barely kept up with inflation…If the state intends to meet the court's standard, the districts contend, it has to spend about 22 percent more than it does now." The problem, a state spokesperson told the *Times*, "is revenue. There's not enough of it. This may be something we're dealing with for many years." For the *Times,* Kentucky's story offered "a cautionary tale of what may lie ahead" for reformers celebrating the recent court victories for fiscal equity in New York."[12]

Sixth, activists have increasingly come to define educational-fiscal "fairness" and "equity" in terms of a minimum bottom for the poorest schools and students and not in the supposedly utopian and unrealistic terms of equality. With state tax revenues dwindling yet further during the last three decades of economic decline, rising wealth concentration, and radically regressive "conservative" political ascendancy, school funding reform advocates have abandoned the struggle for actual school funding equality. They have turned to law suits and legislative proposals seeking nothing more than "adequacy": a modest basic foundational floor that is not worried about ceilings or the replication of private economic hierarchy within public educational allotment systems. "Once upon a time," notes Ellis Cose, "the emphasis [of school funding reform] was on 'equity,' on trying to ensure that the most economically deprived students were provided with resources equal to those lavished on the children of the rich. Now, the cases are about whether the states are providing sufficient resources to poor schools—irrespective of what rich schools get or do not get—to allow students who go to such schools to effectively compete in society. They are called 'adequacy' cases, but they could be more adequately called competency cases since 'they aspire to force states to produce graduates capable of functioning competently as citizens as citizens and as human beings.'"[13]

"Adequate" or "competent" for what? Not to pursue graduate studies in history or medicine or perhaps to become an investment banker on Wall Street. Ability to drive a city bus or handle a cash register or a customer service position would appear to be the basic entitlement. In ordering the provision of extra funds to permit an adequate education in New York City, the New York State Supreme Court made it clear that it was not requiring the provision of a "state of the art" education—the level of educational quality provided to the very disproportionately white children of Manhasset or in the city's own elite private preparatory academies—for the predominantly nonwhite children of the nation's largest city.

The arguably *Brown*-inspired goal of equal funding (the 1954 decision promised educational "equality," not merely "adequacy") is considered hopelessly grandiose and politically unrealistic by practical, hard-headed school-finding reformers, who deride egalitarian funding aspirations as a product of naïve, so-called "Robin Hood" idealism.

Yet even the more realistic struggle for mere funding adequacy seems increasingly beyond reach "given the atrocious budget problems that many states are constantly grappling to resolve" in a climate of regressive, plutocratic tax-cutting. "Unfair school funding is such a large, persistent problem," laments the Education Trust, "that it has the unfortunate air of inevitability. Politicians come and go, blue-ribbon commissions are found and eventually disbanded, lawsuits are filed only to embark on a seemingly endless journey of decision and appeal, and meanwhile another school year begins and low-income and minority children are educated in schools that receive less funding than their peers' wealthier [and whiter] schools. This has gone on for so long that some states have come perilously close to accepting this is as the natural order of things."[14] So it seems in my home state of Illinois, home to the nation's broadest school funding gap, where numerous proposals for reducing the state's high reliance on local property taxes to pay for schools are routinely dismissed by local and state politicians as "politically impossible" even though abundant survey data (including data I have helped generate and analyze) shows that most state residents support equity-enhancing school funding reform.

Seventh, as we have seen, the school quality gap experienced by many black and Latino students is about much more than just school dollars and what they buy. It includes numerous educational and societal practices, mores and ideologies that brand inner-city children of color as inferior and ineducable and justify the selectively harsh imposition of authoritarian, alienating, anti-intellectual, and discipline-centered pedagogies and school cultures on those children.

Eighth, the post-*Brown* fiscal equity (1970s–1980s) and adequacy (since the early 1990s) campaign's focus on money has tended to breed a complex, litigious, and often reactionary debate about "whether money really matters and, if so, how much" in the educational performance (as measured by standardized tests) of segregated minority children. This focus has led—"necessarily," in professor Moran's view—to sticky, time-consuming "concerns about efficiency, concerns that can [and often do] eclipse equity claims."[15] In the complicated quest for school-funding "efficiency," Moran argues, "bureaucratic-managerialist" policy experts and makers "borrow from the business world by likening education to a product process and monitoring it to prevent waste." One such capitalist approach takes an "accounting" perspective by "examin[ing] input measures, tracking expenditures as a form of investment in educational production."

A different "business" method focuses on "accountability," emphasizing "output measures so that quality control can be introduced into the educational system." The key "output measures," of course, are provided by what Moran calls "the technology of standardized, skill-compartmentalized testing." One might expect," Moran elaborates—noting how educational policy wonks postpone serious attention to persistent steep educational opportunity disparities—"that accounting and accountability systems" would be strongly linked to one another by practitioners of the new "business" approach. In reality, however, "there is little serious research linking specific [school-funding] inputs to particular [test-score] outcomes." A "focus on [school-funding] inputs," Moran explains, "can highlight structural problems of inadequate resources, while outcome measures [test-scores] typically mask these difficulties by emphasizing individual factors such as student motivation and teacher effort. Because rural schools and poor, nonwhite urban schools are systematically under-funded, politicians have preferred to use accountability measures test-scores without any detailed accounting of school-funding inputs."

In contemporary school funding deliberations, as throughout the history of capitalist policymaking, "efficiency" concerns are being used to mask privilege and to divert attention from inequality. While there have been recent efforts "to use testing requirements to press for an adequate public education" and make "poor outcomes the basis for demanding additional school resources," these "efforts have yet," Moran notes, "to be translated from scholarly imagining into binding legal precedent."

Lost in this discussion is the toxic role that the great "outcomes"-measuring device—standardized tests—play in perverting the pedagogical practice (an "input" if one likes) of so many of the nation's poor segregated schools. This brings us to an emergent ninth limit to the state-level fiscal equity/adequacy strategy as an effort to deliver on *Brown's* promise: reliance on the reactionary national testing craze to advance the cause of funding reform. Public school equity/adequacy advocates are correct to point out the sharp contradiction between public officials' strident demand that all students and schools (regardless of wealth, race, and other distinctions) perform well on standardized tests and their reluctance and, too often, refusal to provide poor schools with public-educational resources that are adequate to the job of boosting student performance. They are also correct, I think, to suspect that the dark purpose beneath this absurd contradiction—a fundamental problem with the bipartisan George W. Bush administration's No Child Left Behind Act (to be discussed in greater detail in the next two chapters)—is to make public schools more vulnerable to the hard right's real educational agenda: privatization of supposedly "failed schools," many of which are in fact doing the best they can with large numbers of poor and segregated children. By making the corporate testing industry a tool for funding reform, however, such advocates deepen the hold of one part of the total structure of educational apartheid—authoritarian apartheid pedagogy—in order to more effectively (they think) attack another part of that structure: apartheid funding.

This may be self-defeating since the causes of social justice and civic decency, including fair school funding, depend on the existence of highly engaged critical-thinking capacities among those victimized by race, class and other structural inequalities. The testing movement works to kill those capacities.

Tenth, the quest for efficiency for arising from fiscal reformers' focus on money helped open the door to the dangerous call for the dismantling of public education in the name of free market doctrine. Preying on the all-too predictable difficulties experienced by under-funded and high-poverty schools, corporate-neoliberal education strategists and their political allies argue that the public sector is inherently too corrupt, inefficient, inflexible, and/or inept to properly implement—at a reasonable cost—the educational reforms required to lift the nation's failing schools. These educational privatization advocates argue that private management and free-market—that is, corporate—forces will make more efficient use of scarce public resources than the supposedly dysfunctional public bureaucracy. Believing in the presumptive superiority of market forces and (hence) corporate power, school privatization advocates claim that their competition- and choice-based schemes—charter schools, for-profit contract schools (whereby corporations provide support to publicly under-funded schools that agree to sell only their product [e.g. Coke or Pepsi]) or let them place a billboard on a school athletic field—will increase disadvantaged children's access to quality education.[16]

I do not mean to suggest that school funding reform is not a noble, basic, and essential cause to be embraced and pursued by one and all reformers who are serious about making *Brown's* promise come to life in the twenty-first century. Increased funding is, I think, necessary but in itself insufficient for meaningful improvement in the educational experience of apartheid's child victims. I would be remiss if I did not conclude this chapter by noting the rich moral obscenity that lay at the heart of the notion that we should even be discussing "whether money matters" for poor children and under-funded schools while we dole out hundreds of billions of dollars for the noble causes of militarism, empire, corporate welfare, and tax cuts for the already super-opulent few in the industrialized world's most unequal and wealth-top-heavy nation.

It is one thing, and quite correct, to say that officially adequate or even equalized school funding in and of itself cannot deliver equal educational opportunity for the nation's millions of poor and truly disadvantaged children of color. It is another thing to say that the absence of solid proof showing that more money quickly and clearly translates into heightened minority student test-score outcomes indicates that savage school funding inequalities can be indefinitely tolerated. This is what a leading education reporter for the *Chicago Tribune* suggested to me in January of 2003, after I spoke (in my role as the research director of an urban black civil rights organization) at a press conference giving the results of a statewide opinion survey showing that the majority of the state's politically attentive residents supported a significant, equity-enhancing reform of the state's public educational finance system. Test scores, this reporter knew, are most closely correlated in the existing academic literature, to socioeconomic status—low scores being linked to high poverty and high scores being linked to low poverty. Those scores are not strongly linked to school funding differences. Since the racial-ethnic achievement gap is not irrefutably correlated with the school funding gap in the official (but rather sparse) research on the issue to date, this journalist told me, my predominantly black organization's civil-rights case for school funding reform was tenuous at best.

Money doesn't really matter in determining the quality of education children receive? Then surely the more affluent, well-equipped, and predominantly white suburban school districts and elite private schools will be happy to sacrifice their steep fiscal advantages, handing over their surplus school dollars to struggling children and teachers in highly impoverished communities. Certainly, then, the preservers of race and class privilege are prepared to test the thesis that educational and school success is really just about hard and honest work, moral discipline—a "culture of achievement" and "accountability" and not inherited and structural advantage, station, and resources—by letting their excess youth-instructional cash and all that goes with it (the best schools, the latest instructional technologies, the highest-paid and most qualified teachers, the latest materials, the ample auditoriums, playing fields and libraries, and more) flow back to the disadvantaged schools and communities that struggle in the forgotten shadows of the great central-city corporate downtowns that provide the economic basis for the safe, sheltered, and pleasing lives and campuses enjoyed by richer white suburbanites. Since educational money isn't really relevant, then surely the Lake Forests, Great Necks, Grosse Points, Manhassets, and Andover and Marin Academies of America are willing to see the provision of educational resources properly aligned with the need for such resources.

As Peter Schrag argues with eloquence at the end of a chapter in which he reviews academics' and policy wonk's complex debate over what affluent Ivy League and Rand Corporation researchers call "the relationship between student performance and school resources":[17]

> No parent or student should have to offer scientific proof that attractive schools with working toilets and decent classroom environments are more productive than those without. None should be asked how they knew that having rats in their classrooms impaired their ability to learn. Nor should any school have to justify good libraries and after-school programs in art or music with test scores and college attendance rates. What's perfectly clear is that when people can afford it, they opt for the schools with rich resources, and often struggle (and sometimes lie and cheat) to get their children into the right schools.

This excellent statement is consistent with Kozol's powerful comment (see chapter two) on "questions that are seldom posed when wealthy people contemplate the benefits of sending their own children to expensive private schools or when they move to exclusive suburbs in which public schools are spending more than twice what public schools in the South Bronx are spending on their children." It is consistent also with the judgment of the New Jersey Supreme Court in 1990, when school funding reform advocates were still interested in pushing for funding equality. After noting the remarkable school advantages that richer districts purchased at often "staggering" expense, the New Jersey Court that decided the *Abbott II* case asked an interesting question: "If these factors were not related to quality of education, why are the richer districts willing to spend so much on them?"

As for the *Tribune* reporter's test-score-based challenge to the cause of school funding reform, here is the answer I gave to her (and to the notion that inefficient spending practices by urban schools mean that city schools should not receive adequate funding) during an urban "education summit" held at Robert Clemente High School, on the near West Side of Chicago, in February of 2004:[18]

> It's not entirely clear that there's no significant correlation between resources and scores. I doubt that it is a purely accidental coincidence that Illinois has both the biggest school funding gap and the biggest achievement gap between rich and impoverished students.
>
> But there doesn't have to be a perfect or even a strong correlation to make the cause for funding equity in Illinois. In most of the relevant state-level school funding case law to date, it's about equal educational opportunity not equal test-score outcomes. It's acknowledged that a whole slew of factors go into the achievement gap and that the research is unclear and contested about the precise relationship between school funding and achievement.

Take it out of the court room and the seminar room and think about it like a parent whose got two kids, one of whom is thriving and the other one of whom is struggling with growing up, including their ABCs. You certainly wouldn't decide, at least I hope you wouldn't, to not give the struggling kid equal attention and food and clothes and resources. You wouldn't predicate their share of family wealth on performance-based outcomes, as a matter of family policy. You don't take slow Jennifer and put her in the basement and ban her from the library and the Internet and give fast Johnny the best bedroom and full access to the learning resources in the house.

It's certainly true that overall community and family poverty—low "socioeconomic status," to use the social science language—provides the leading correlation with test-score "failure." But let's think for a minute about a useful analogy. Do you give fewer funds for street lights to a certain town because that community tends to have a large number of bad sunspot intersections where it's hard to make out the lights? The better response would be to increase the stoplight expenditures there to include special anti-glare mechanisms and techniques—to pay for the special stoplight and traffic extras required in a bad glare community.

If the school funding money isn't going as far we would like in, say Chicago, it may well be that—as many critics say—the money is not being spent wisely or fairly by the Chicago Public Schools. It isn't, say, being targeted in a way that properly matches the special barriers prevalent in inner city schools. Ok, fine, so you examine that and invest accordingly. You don't say, "forget it, its all over for you … we're going to kill you with un-funded mandates and sadistic testing regimens until we pick you off with vouchers and turn it all over to Edison and the religious schools."

You don't say that, that is, if you are serious about reforming and sustaining the common public school. If you are genuine on that score, then there's no good reason to set up harsh either/or black and white dichotomies between more efficient spending and more equitable spending.

And it's interesting that the whole "do more with less" line is directed mainly at minority urban schools and not at the richer districts where there's certainly equivalent waste that gets covered up by overall socioeconomic and related cultural advantages that tend to ensure decent test scores.

Of course, the real experiment to prove that school funding inequality is not a big factor in the achievement gap would be to practice full funding equity for a generation or two—or more. After all, we've been practicing savage school funding inequality for more than a hundred years.

Having cautiously but firmly embraced the cause of school funding reform, this book will now turn to the harsh overall socioeconomic and related cultural inequalities that significantly impact educational experience from beyond school walls. These powerful disparities challenge any attempt to fulfill *Brown*'s promise—or even *Plessy*'s promise—that is not accompanied by, and linked to, significant broad social reform.

4

THE DEEPER INEQUALITY

Attempting to fix inner city schools without fixing the city in which they are embedded is like trying to clear the air on one side of a city door…Educational change in the inner city, to be successful, has to be part and parcel of more fundamental social change.

—Jean Anyon, 1997[1]

Where students come to class hungry, exhausted, or afraid, when they bounce from school to school as their families face eviction, where they have no one at home to wake them up for the bus, much less look over their homework, not even the best-equipped facilities, the strongest curricula, and the best-paid teacher can ensure success.

—Gary Orfield, 2001[2]

Schools and teachers are not responsible for the economic and family problems that are the sources of the deepest indignities afflicting many inner-city children. Yet schools, historically, are the public institutions we have most relied upon to heal the wounds imposed by inequalities in more private spheres.

—Jeffrey Henig, 1999[3]

School reform is not enough. In seeking to close the achievement gap for low-income and minority students, policy makers focus inordinate attention on the improvement of instruction because they apparently believe that social class differences are immutable and that only schools can improve the destinies of lower-class children. This is a peculiarly American belief—that schools can be virtually the only instrument of social reform.

—Richard Rothstein, 2004[4]

You know, there's a lot of talk about how to keep the economy growing. We talk about fiscal matters. But perhaps the best way to keep jobs here in America and to keep the economy growing is to make sure our education system works. I went to Washington to solve problems.... No, education is how to help the person who's lost a job. Education is how to make sure we've got a workforce that's productive and competitive.

—George W. Bush, Presidential Debates, October 2004[5]

RAYOLA'S STORY: TO UPTOWN AND BACK

In the summer of 2004, more than four months after the bittersweet celebration of Brown's fiftieth anniversary, the *Chicago Tribune* told the cautionary tale of a third-grader named Rayola Carwell. During a ten-month period in the 2002–2003 school year, *Tribune* reporter Stephanie Banchero observed Rayola at school and at home and conducted numerous interviews with Rayola's teachers, principals, and family members. The ostensible point of the story, presented as a three-part series, was to highlight the difficulty that Chicago public school students face when they attempt to utilize the transfer provision of the 2001 No Child Left Behind Act (NCLB).[6] In the process of detailing problems with NCLB-implementation, however, Banchero painted a broader and deeper portrait of the many interrelated educational obstacles faced by a young black girl from an especially poor, marginalized, and hyper-segregated ghetto neighborhood. Many of these barriers to learning originate outside schools, largely beyond the reach of educational staff, authorities, and policy.

Rayola's Neighborhood: "A Community That Is Slowly Dying"

During the year covered by Banchero, Rayola lived with two brothers, a grandmother, an aunt, and a cousin in a rented five-bedroom house in the poor and dangerous South Side neighborhood of Englewood. In 1999, according to the U.S. Census, Englewood was 98 percent African American, making it one of twenty-two 90 percent or more black neighborhoods that together house nearly three-fourths (74 percent) of the black population in a city that contains seventy-seven neighborhoods. Median household income in Englewood in 1999 was $18, 955, less than 28 percent of median household income ($68,613) in the 85 percent white North Side Chicago neighborhood of Lincoln Park and less than 39 percent of the Economic Policy Institute's painstaking calculation of the minimum basic annual family budget for a household comprised of two adults and three children in 1999.[7] More than one-fourth of Englewood's eligible adult workers were officially unemployed and 40 percent of the neighborhood's residents, including 55 percent of its children, were officially poor under the federal government's insufficiently low definition of poverty.

Just less that one-third (31.3 percent) of Englewood's children lived in what social researchers call "deep poverty"—at less than half of that miserly poverty rate. A roughly equivalent percentage (30.5 percent) of the neighborhood's children received public family cash assistance (Temporary Assistance for Needy Families, formerly known as Aid for Families with Dependent Children) in a community where nearly one-third of the households were headed by single mothers officially mired in poverty and 40 percent of the adults were high school dropouts.[8]

These statistics, it is worth noting, are hardly the worst neighborhood-specific socioeconomic indicators that could be found among the aforementioned twenty-two neighborhoods in the 2000 Census.[9] They came, moreover, at the peak of the longest peacetime economic expansion in post-World War II American history (the long "Clinton boom" of the 1990s) and before the onset of an economic slowdown that by 2002 pushed black Chicagoans' employment-population ratio (the percentage of all adult blacks attached to the labor market) below 50 percent.

In an elaborate multi-factor analysis that gave each of the city's seventy-seven neighborhoods a composite "economic vitality" score, Englewood ranked fifth from the bottom.[10] When students from Chicago and Loyola Universities accompanied me on field visits to Englewood on repeated occasions in the spring of 2004, we observed a large number of teen and younger adult males gathering on street corners. Some of these "unattached youth" were clearly enrolled in gang organizations and visibly engaged in the narcotics trade. Older and presumably unemployed males could be seen congregating around ubiquitous liquor stores, missions, and empty lots. The endemic stress, disappointment, and danger of inner-city life was etched on residents' faces. Equally evident was the relative absence of retail facilities, services, and institutions that are standard in the city's richer, whiter neighborhoods: full-service modern grocery stores, drugstores, bookstores, restaurants, doctors, dentists, lawyers, dry-cleaners, banks, personal investment and family insurance stores, tax consultants, boutiques, coffee shops, and much more. Businesses and homes were visibly dilapidated on many blocks, with many of the former relying on hand-painted signs to advertise their wares. Boarded up homes and business were widely evident, as were broken-down cars. Local business owners protected their enterprises from burglary with bars and gated shutters. Pawnshops and barebones storefront churches were widely visible, as were liquor stores, often combined with small groceries, and currency exchanges advertising super-exploitive payday loans. Taxicabs and newspaper boxes or stands were practically nonexistent.

The small number of whites seen in these neighborhoods were males working in traditional working-class "jobs that pay" (street and sewer repair, construction trades, police officers, and firemen)—jobs in which blacks have long been underrepresented. Police cars cruised warily, their occupants donning bullet-proof vests deemed necessary in waging the war on drugs in neighborhoods where people with felony records outnumber those with legitimate jobs. Many intersections and blocks on the west side were subject to around-the-clock surveillance by rotating elevated police cameras placed atop telephone poles in officially designated high-crime areas.

DePaul University student Ralph Edwards offered the following reflections:[11]

When traveling through the Englewood community you are hit with the harsh reality that poverty exists in the United States of America. You see a place that is depleted and under-developed. You see in a poor black neighborhood *a Third World country* [emphasis added]...

You see countless open lots in this neighborhood. You will come across a setting where there is one house, right beside it an open lot, on the side of that another house, and then [another] open lot. Some of the homes you observe are kept up just enough to get by, while the next house seems like it would be better off as an open lot. You see homes with broken windows and boarded-up windows and local residents living in the compounds of the homes.

Besides the homes I observed there is little real businesses in the area. There is an Osco and a couple of Walgreen pharmacies. All the other businesses were chain restaurants, small proprietors, single chain food stores, and dollar stores. The only thing that outnumbered single proprietor chain stores were storefront churches. There were over 80 storefront churches in this community. In one stretch of road there were over 16 storefront churches, next to liquor stores, Burger Kings...There were not many dentists or doctors. There were a few clinics and a couple of Osco pharmacies. This alone made me wonder what is being done to really help people in the community. You observe there are not many Laundromats or really full-service grocery stores, where people have a chance to buy quality food.

When I look at Englewood, I see a community that is slowly dying if someone does not step in and give back to the people...just look at the number of small businesses that do not help. They are as dilapidated and run down as the homes in the community...you see trash all over the place.

If you go a little further to different parts of Chicago you see that life is a lot different. In the upper class neighborhoods you do not see storefront churches, hundreds of Ma and Pa grocery and liquor stores and currency exchanges, run down homes and bad roads. In the upper-class neighborhoods you only see one or two fast food restaurants, but instead you see a lot of restaurants in which you can bring your family to come in and eat. When you ride through an upper class neighborhood you see nice buildings and nice streets....

I know first hand that something like a 24-hour grocery store such as Dominick's or Jewel will help a community like Englewood or North Lawndale grow. If you want these communities to prosper you must find a way to give them more opportunities and jobs. People would not be hanging on street corners in these communities if you give them something to live for ... Take a chance to put some banks up and give people a chance to get loans to fix up their homes. Unless some person, organization, or institution invests the time and money into minority neighborhoods they will not have a chance catching up to their counterparts in the upper class neighborhoods.

The author of these comments counted "at least seven" currency exchanges, twenty-seven liquor stores, sixty-two small retail stores (mainly with hand-painted signs), fourteen empty lots, sixty-two dilapidated buildings, three health clinics, no doctors' office, thirty-one smaller food and convenience stores, two open green spaces, and more than eighty storefront churches during a drive through Englewood.[12]

Rayola's Mother and Her Dream

With the city's second highest crime rate in 2002, Englewood is so gang-ridden that Rayola's mother Yolanda Carwell forbade her children from playing out-of-doors. "I always walked with my brother," Rayola told Banchero, "because of the bad guys standing outside."[13]

Yolanda, thirty-two, was a single mother of three and a high-school drop out. She had "spent her life moving from one low-paying job to another, boxing chicken at KFC, working as a security guard and driving patients to their doctor's appointments." She left high school at seventeen because she "thought school was a waste of time." By age twenty-two, Banchero noted, Yolanda was "living in public housing and pregnant with her second child Rayola. Now," Banchero observed, "she has three children by two men and says she has to fight for child support payments." Rayola's family moved at least six times in ten years. On some occasions, these moves took place "just as eviction notices were arriving." Yolanda told Banchero, "I never got to live my dreams. I want my kids to live theirs."

In pursuit of that goal in the summer of 2003, Yolanda tried to take advantage of the NCLB's "transfer provision" to move Rayola out of her neighborhood school in Englewood. She participated in a citywide drawing whereby children attending the city's large number of "failing schools" (as determined by low test-scores) vied through a lottery to be permitted to transfer to "successful" schools.

Rayola attended second grade at Holmes Elementary, "an uninviting gray-brick building bordered by vacant lots and a boarded-up house." Holmes' entrance "opens onto Garfield Boulevards, a street that forms a gauntlet of drug-dealing and other crimes. Behind the school, a small playground sits in the middle of a cracked concrete parking lot." Thanks to years of abysmally low student standardized test scores, Holmes was officially designated a "failed school," one whose students are eligible, under the NCLB, to switch to a school within their district that boasted a better test-score record.

Holmes, it is worth noting, was the fourth school Rayola had attended by the fall of 2003. There are many depressing, low-scoring schools like Holmes throughout the hundreds of ghetto poverty census tracts that are stitched together across the predominantly black, hyper-segregated stretches of the west and south sides of Chicago, recently anointed as one of the world's fifteen "global cities."[14]

Like She "Won The Lottery": Rayola's New School

The new school to which Yolanda sent Rayola in August 2003 was located thirteen miles northeast, in the racially integrated but increasingly gentrified North Side Chicago neighborhood of Uptown. The community surrounding Rayola's new school—Stockton Elementary—"is a prime draw," Banchero noted, "for young urban professionals, with renovated homes selling for $600,000 or more and upscale bistros doing brisk business." In contrast to the neo-Dickensian, slum-situated spectacle of Holmes, Banchero observed, "Stockton is a bright, three-story, red-brick building on a tree-lined street. A black wrought-iron fence encloses a trimmed lawn and a colorful bed of wildflowers, daisies and azalea bushes. Vibrant mosaics of children frolicking and studying enliven the space above the schools' doors." The descriptive contrast with Holmes suggests some of what Jonathan Kozol means when he writes about the "aesthetic" dimensions of modern educational apartheid. As far as Yolanda was concerned, initially, Rayola had "won the lottery" when she was allowed to transfer to Stockton.

Where Holmes was 100 percent African American in 2003–2004, Stockton was 38 percent black, 9 percent white, 46 percent Latino and 7 percent "other," primarily Asian. There were 23.4 students for every teacher at Holmes, compared to 17 students per teacher at Stockton. Fourteen percent of Holmes' classes were taught by teachers "considered not highly qualified." Fifty-six percent of Stockton's students met Illinois test-score standards, compared to just 30 percent at Holmes. The former school's scores had tripled and its reading scores doubled since 1996.[15] That was the year that Stockton was taken over by Principal Deborah Esperza, a dynamic former corporate systems consultant who "rocketed through the teaching ranks in four years." Esperza, Banchero noted, "knows that the state test scores are the primary factor in whether her school is labeled a success or a failure by the federal government."

Esperza certainly also knew that the Chicago Public School system (CPS) does not hesitate to brand low-scoring schools as "failures" and, in some cases, to shut such schools down. Just weeks before the *Tribune* series on Rayola appeared, in fact, the CPS announced that it would be closing sixty "failed" (chronically low-scoring) schools in predominantly black neighborhoods on the city's south and west sides over the next six years. Under the city's ambitious "Renaissance 2010" Plan, the closings will be accompanied by the creation of one hundred new and smaller schools that will stress "personalized curricula" and more intimate interaction between students, teachers, and staff. Just one-third of the reconstituted schools will still be managed by the district. The remainder will be charters or contract schools run by independent organizations, including for-profit corporations in the contract schools. Principles, teachers, and other staff in most of the closed schools will have no guarantee of re-hire and many of the new schools will be run on a newly nonunion basis. The plan was announced and introduced with minimal input from parents, community, teachers, and staff, none of whom qualified alongside private corporations and certain selected academic think-tanks as "experts" to be tapped by the city for significant advice on how to reform the city's schools.[16]

The Failed Transfer

Rayola's transfer to Esperza's successful Uptown school didn't work out, thanks in part to the sheer distance and difficulty of the commute between Englewood and Uptown. Yolanda initially explored the possibility of renting a three-bedroom apartment in the North Side neighborhood. But even a two-bedroom apartment in that rapidly gentrifying community was beyond her financial reach. A rental opportunity in Uptown was nixed when a landlord told Yolanda that he required a security deposit of $1,610. Things might have worked out if the Carwell family could have received a state grant for which it was eligible—an allowance that would have paid the deposit and the first three months of rent. Social workers at Stockton worked hard to make this happen, but "the plans were dashed" when Yolanda failed to complete the necessary paperwork.

By mid-November of 2003, Rayola had missed fourteen of Stockton's first forty-six school days and been late for another twelve. Her poor attendance put her dangerously behind in the critical third grade. The learning difficulties she experienced had nothing, her teachers agreed, to do with a lack of native intelligence or willingness to do her work: Rayola was both smart and hard-working, the instructors reported. The biggest problem was missed time resulting from long commutes that were often impossible because Yolanda had to work in the morning and there was nobody available to drive her daughter across town. There were problems also with meeting the costs of the commute. Yolanda received a $191 transportation subsidy under the NCLB, but nine weeks into the school year she was forced to use this stipend to pay for food and rent and Rayola missed a few school days as the family van was out of gas.

In many cases, however, Rayola missed school because her mother let her and her brothers stay up late watching television and failed to wake them up the next morning. To make matters worse, Rayola often came to school without breakfast, which she missed in the rush created by the time squeeze produced by sleeping in and the long trip to Stockton.

Back to the South Side

Concerned that the likely poor test-score performance of Rayola and other children who transferred to Stockton under the NCLB might undercut her school's cherished status as a skill-and-drill "success," Esperza confronted Yolanda on the need to get Rayola to school on time. After initially denying the problem and then considering a bus-driving job that might have permitted her to deliver Rayola to Stockton at the appropriate hour, Yolanda gave up on her dream of sending Rayola to the North Side school.

On the seventy-sixth day of the school year, she enrolled Rayola in another 100 percent black South Side school—Attucks Elementary. Yolanda claimed to have chosen Attucks because the CPS Web site had listed it as a "high-performing school," but the CPS actually listed it as a school whose students did so poorly that it needed to let them transfer out under the NCLB. Rayola went from seventeen classmates per one teacher and one tutor at Stockton to twenty-five students per one teacher and no tutor at Attucks. She continued to miss a large number of school days due to late-night television and sleeping in. But the less demanding nature of the curriculum and assignments at Attucks made it easy for Rayola to catch up with her fellow students and her end-of-the-year test scores were good enough to graduate.

Her mother pulled her out of Attucks two weeks before the end of the school years so that the family could "visit relatives in Michigan." The visit did not take place. Yolanda told Banchero she wasn't sure why she removed Rayola before the end of the semester, confiding that "sometimes I do things and shock myself... right now, I'm saying, 'why did I do that?'"

THE LONG SHADOW OF COLEMAN

NCLB Implementation and Educational Apartheid

The story of Rayola Carwell's struggle to attain "a sound and basic education" touches upon numerous problems that have long vexed educational activists, researchers, and policymakers in the *Brown* and post-*Brown* eras. It also highlights some very specific difficulties with the NCLB. As is so often in the history of school desegregation, the least advantaged, not the more advantaged child had to bear the primary travel and related time burden imposed by residential and educational apartheid.[17] Since Yolanda could not afford to live in the more affluent vicinity of Stockton (much less Lake Forest), it was up to the ghettoized Carwells to get themselves to the site of increased educational opportunity. It was not up to the educational authorities to bring better school quality to the hypersegregated Carwells.

When it comes to getting Rayola and her inner-city cohorts to quality schools, however, the heavily racialized city-suburban split that worried Thurgood Marshall poses a strong barrier to success. In a study released in December of 2004, the Illinois Facilities Fund reported that 157,000 elementary school children in twenty Chicago neighborhoods had a less than one in five chance of "going to a nearby [local/neighborhood] school" where at least 40 percent of the students met state testing standards. These neighborhoods were very disproportionately concentrated on the city's black South and West sides.[18] With *four hundred* city schools on the federal government's "needs improvement" list, there were only 1,000 transfer slots open within the city for the 19,000 Chicago kids whose parents requested NCLB transfers from failed to successful schools in 2003–2004. In 2004–2005, the CPS predicted, there would be just 457 slots for 30,000 transfer-eligible kids. The city's racially balanced "magnet" schools, high-quality institutions specially designed to stem white and middle-class flight to the suburbs, are exempted from accepting such transfers.[19] To significantly improve the chances that students like Rayola could attend high-performing schools, the federal government would probably have to encourage and significantly fund transfers to more affluent suburban districts—something that isn't remotely contemplated under the NCLB.

The government also fails to adequately support NCLB transfer-students once they've arrived at high-performance schools. Once students like Rayola make it to more successful schools like Stockton (itself nowhere near as successful as the standard elementary school in the white suburbs) with help from transportation subsidies, the law provides no additional dollars to help bring those students up to the level of their new classmates. "I think we can all agree that every child should have access to the best schools," Esperza told Banchero, "but it is short-sighted not to provide extra money to help the students once they get here."[20]

What, however, about adequately funding and improving the schools in which the great majority of inner-city students will be stuck, rather than dreaming up avenues of escape for the lucky few who can transfer out? Reflecting on the reluctance of white suburbanites to open their doors to the inner-city children seeking transfers under the NCLB, the liberal Education Trust's Policy Director Ross Weiner argues that policymakers face the "challenge…of communicating with the public to make all of us concerned with the education of everyone's children. There are far too many children," Weiner elaborates, "assigned to schools that aren't serving them. If we say there aren't enough other places for them to go, we have to be committed to making their [current] schools better." For Weiner's organization, this commitment requires school funding reform and equity, combined with the standards-based school improvement designed to convince wary taxpayers that "more money will transfer into more student learning."[21]

Coleman, Jencks, and the Deeper Inequality

I agree with Weiner and other school reformers on the need for efficiently run and adequately and fairly funded schools that might more adequately serve inner-city students like Rayola. At the same time, in reading the *Tribune* series on Rayola, I also found myself flashing back to the famous 1966 "Coleman Report." Written in response to the 1964 Civil Rights Act's requirement that the federal government conduct a study "concerning the lack of availability of equal educational opportunity for individuals by reasons of race, color, religion, or national origin," sociologist James Coleman's 737-page report, accompanied by 548 pages of statistical explanation and based on data from thousands of teachers and students, ended up refuting the notion that difference in school resources was the major reason for disparities in black and white educational achievement.[22]

Coleman's study unexpectedly and fundamentally challenged the core liberal American notion that, in Godfrey Hodgson's words, "education was the high road to equality." According to Hodgson's 1976 analysis, this notion holds special attraction for Americans because it appeals to their historical preference of "equality of opportunity" over the more socialistic principle of "equality of condition." It means "giving a chance to the have-nots" that "the haves do not notice losing." It also appeals to the "tradition of Protestantism and the ethic of self-improvement that stretches back down the American tradition through Horatio Alger and McGruff's *Readers* to Benjamin Franklin."[23]

The notion that schools were the avenue to social equality has a long history that both predates and survives the Coleman report. As Jeffrey Henig has more recently noted, "schools and teachers are not responsible for the economic and family problems that are the sources of the deepest indignities afflicting many inner-city children. Yet schools, historically, are the public institutions we have most relied upon to heal the wounds imposed by inequalities in more private spheres."[24]

Much to the surprise and disappointment of those who looked, in the American tradition, to schools as the answer to the burning (literally, often enough) issues of racial inequality in 1960s America, Coleman's report concluded that racial differences in school resources held no statistically relevant relationship to racial differences in test-measured academic performance. For Coleman, the biggest achievement-separating and suppressing factors were broadly socioeconomic and sociologically environmental, including parents' income and educational levels, home experience, and peer culture. These extra-school factors, Coleman determined, were a much bigger determinant of black children's educational experience and performance than anything schools were doing or not doing. Deeper inequalities of socioeconomic status, Coleman concluded, accounted for 66–80 percent of educational achievement as gauged by the standard measures of the time.[25] For Coleman, the most relevant parts of Rayola's struggle to learn would have more to do with her home and ghetto neighborhood environment than with any differences in quality or funding between Holmes and Stockton. Pleased to note that Holmes actually spent more per student than Stockton in 2002–2003,[26] Coleman would focus instead on the stressful danger and poverty of her neighborhood, the chaos of her single-parent household, the absence of successful educated role models in her home and community, the missed breakfasts, the lack of privacy, and absence of books in her home and of bookstores and libraries in her community, the ubiquitous late-night blare of the television, and the struggle of her intermittently employed, dropout mother—unable or unwilling to enforce reasonable sleeping and studying patterns for her children.

According to sociologist Chrisopher Jencks, in his controversial 1972 book *Inequality: A Reassessment of the Effect of Family and Schooling in America,* Coleman's report gave the lie to the (he felt) not-so-egalitarian liberal American political tradition. When most Americans claim to embrace equality, Jencks argued, what they really supported was just "equality of opportunity," not "equality of condition." For Jencks, however, the Coleman report and the failed social reforms of the 1960s showed that the only way to increase equality of opportunity, including educational opportunity, was *precisely to increase equality of socioeconomic condition* in the here and now—something that required direct political intervention against the systematic poverty-generating concentration of economic power in capitalist America. "As long as egalitarians assume that public policy cannot contribute to economic equality directly, but must proceed by ingenious manipulation of *marginal institutions like schools* [emphasis added]," Jencks warned, "progress will remain glacial. If we want to move beyond this tradition," Jencks declared, "we will have to establish political control over the economic institutions that shape our society. This is what other countries call socialism. Anything less will end in the same disappointments as the reforms of the 1960s."[27]

After a thorough review of the relevant literature and statistics, including Coleman's own exhaustive data sets, Jencks determined that no amount of school reform and funding equity—not even the full compensatory inversion of existing school resource disparities—could overcome the educational consequences of the deeper social inequality. While he was uncomfortable with discussing schools as "factories" (a common metaphor in the educational literature of the 1960s and 1970s), Jencks made a chilling industrial analogy. "It is true," he argued, "that schools have 'inputs' and 'outputs' and that one of their nominal purposes is to take human 'raw materials' (i.e., children) and convert them into something 'valuable' (i.e., employable adults). Our research suggests, however, that the characteristics of a school's output depend largely on a single input, namely the children. Everything else—the school budget, its policies, the characteristics of the teachers—is either secondary or completely irrelevant."

That critical student "input," Jencks argued, was "much more influenced by what happens at home than what happens in school. They may also be more influenced by what happens on the streets and by what they see on television." Significantly, Jencks found that "utilization of school resources was even more unequal than access to them": the biggest disparity was about willingness and ability to exploit whatever educational quality was provided. Urban middle-class families, Jencks had argued in 1969, tend to "nourish academic skills and interests" among children but lower-class life "does the opposite."[28]

Jencks' industrial analogy contrasts with Roy L. Brooks' more recent computer-age metaphor in his discussion of what's needed to improve segregated inner-city schools. "Money," Brooks wrote in 1996, is "the hardware of the educational enterprise; academic programming is the software. Without the latter, all the gold in Fort Knox will not improve educational performance."[29] Where, one might well ask, is the vital circulating human capital of the student "raw material" in this analogy? All the school funding "gold" *and* cutting edge educational programming software, a contemporary Coleman might argue, won't buy significantly improved educational and related longer term socioeconomic outcomes for the majority of inner-city children if not accompanied by a reduction in poverty and its many terrible effects on those children within and beyond school walls.

"Failed Schools" or Failed Society?

A perfect example, many think, is provided by the tragic story of the Kansas City public schools. Between 1986 and 2002, Kansas City officials responded to a judge's order to fix its broken, highly segregated, predominantly black, and racially isolated schools by spending $2 billion on public education and introducing a measure of school choice within the city schools. Thanks to this spectacular urban-educational spending spree, the city's schools by the end of the twentieth century were "packed with extraordinary goodies. At [Kansas City's] Central High School alone," the *Los Angeles Times* reported, "there are 900 top-of-the-line computers, an Olympic size swimming pool with six diving boards, a padded wrestling room, a classical Greek theater, an eight-lane indoor track, and a gymnastic center stocked with professional equipment. The districts' sky's-the-limit buying blitz," the *Times* noted, "loaded its schools with luxuries ranging from a planetarium to a recording studio to a 100-acre farm, from philosophy teachers for 7th-graders to a world-class Romanian fencing coach who took his high-school athletes to matches in Europe and Africa."[30]

In 2000, the Kansas City school districts became the first big-city district ever to lose its accreditation after it flunked all of Missouri's performance standards. As Harvard Civil Rights Project Director Gary Orfield noted in the preface to Alison Morantz's detailed study of what went wrong in Kansas City, "if simply funneling large amounts of money and choice into a system can produce large educational gains, we should see them in Kansas City." Morantz's study, carried out under Orfield's direction, found no evidence that concentrated compensatory investments in urban education produced achievement gains for minority students. What went wrong?

Two years after its publication, Brooks cited this study as proof that more school-funding can't improve inner-city education unless it is accompanied by improved academic programming. In fact, however, Morantz's study had nothing to say about academic programming per se. She focused her criticism on the Kansas City desegregation plan's failure to include the entire metropolitan area in its magnet-schools-based effort to address educational apartheid and on the (she felt) dysfunctional way the plan was funded. In May of 2001, moreover, her director Gary Orfield explained the Kansas City fiasco to the *Los Angeles Times* in rather Coleman-esque terms. According to *Times* reporter Stephanie Simon:[31]

> To Orfield, the lesson from Kansas City is clear: money can't buy good schools. Not, at least, in shattered urban districts,

where poverty leaves many children ill-equipped to learn. Where students come to class hungry, exhausted, or afraid, when they bounce from school to school as their families face eviction, where they have no one at home to wake them up for the bus, much less look over their homework, not even the best-equipped facilities, the strongest curricula, and the best-paid teacher can ensure success, he argues. "Basically, we have a huge social crisis, and the schools can't solve it by themselves," Orfield said.

Minus the explicit call for political intervention against private wealth concentration, Orfield sounded like Jencks (circa 1972) on the limits of what schools can really do in a context of broad socioeconomic hierarchy and related concentrated black socioeconomic misery.

Such Coleman-esque sentiments are reasonably widespread among those who pay serious attention to urban schooling issues. In a provocative 2000 cover story titled "What No School Can Do," *New York Times Magazine* education writer James Traub noted that New York City public school students had scored on the latest round of standardized tests in almost perfect accord with their differential poverty rates. The city's mostly "dreadful" test scores "provided fuel," Traub observed "for those who felt that New York City schools are under-financed, that the city uses too many uncertified teachers, that academic standards are low, that junior high schools are neglected, and the tests themselves are unfair. There's some merit in all these notions," Traub acknowledged. But:

What was not said ... was the obvious: that the City districts that performed poorly, like those that performed well, scored almost exactly as the socioeconomic status of the children in them would have predicted. You could have predicted the fourth-grade test-scores of all but one of the

City's 32 districts merely by knowing the percentage of students in a given district who qualified for a free lunch. Only a few dozen of the city's 675 elementary schools scored well despite high poverty rates. In other words, good schools aren't doing that much good and bad schools aren't doing that much harm. This is the case in virtually every big city in the country.

"A child living in an inner city neighborhood," Traub added, "is in school for only so many hours. It's the rest of the day—as well as the rest of the neighborhood—that's the big influence, and the problem—a judgment that provides some context for understanding why some urban school reform programs call for lengthening the school day from early in the morning until the early evening." [32]

Traub could have cited Jean Anyon's chilling reflection on the deep, many sided learning obstacles faced by ghettoized children just across the Hudson River in Newark, New Jersey. Based on her experience as a teaching staff-developer and "school reform coach" at Newark's inner-city "Marcy School" during the early 1990s, Anyon concluded that no serious effort to significantly reform inner-city schools and to improve the educational experience of poor and minority urban children could succeed if it was not connected to and accompanied by sweeping broad social, economic, and political reform. "Attempting to fix inner city schools without fixing the city in which they are embedded," Anyon argued in her widely read book *Ghetto Schooling*, "is like trying to clear the air on one side of a screen door…The recalcitrance of urban schools to 'reform,'" Anyon determined, "is in large part a result of economic and political devastation in the cities.…Educational change in the inner city, to be successful," Anyon learned, "has to be part and parcel of more fundamental social change. An all-out attack on poverty and racial isolation that by necessity will affect not only the poor but the more affluent as well," she concluded, "will be necessary in order to remove the barriers that currently stand in the way of urban educational change."

The "economic and political devastation" of black Newark, Anyon showed, was a deeply rooted historical process that long predated the famous—among public-educational fiscal-equity advocates—*Abbott II* decision (1990) and the subsequent onset of serious, newly (and quite well-) funded reform efforts in the 1990s. Newark had been losing key social and economic resources since the 1930s, Anyon showed. Between the end of World War II and 1970, the city filled up with hundreds of thousands of poorly educated blacks fleeing southern poverty even as corporations were disinvesting in the once industrially robust community. Whites flocked to the city's suburbs. State and federal politicians lost interest in the increasingly isolated, segregated, and deeply poor residents of the increasingly hyper-ghettoized post-industrial city, home to one of the bloodiest race riots of the 1960s. By the early 1970s, as education equity activists first initiated *Brown*-inspired efforts to desegregate and otherwise improve minority educational opportunities in New Jersey, merely educational reforms were already "too little, too late." Newark had become politically "irrelevant" as wealth, population, and organized political clout moved from the forgotten ex-industrial municipality to the burgeoning and very disproportionately white suburban legislative districts.

Anyon hardly turned a blind eye to the savage school-specific funding and other educational inequalities that disfigured educational experience in New Jersey. She did not deny the need for effective transformation in school-programming and the role—unduly negative and shaming, by her observation—that teachers, principals, and other school staff played in the "mis-education" of inner-city children. She quoted at length from an outside evaluators' description of the city schools' "dirty and ill-equipped" classrooms, "unchallenging and often misguided and inappropriate instruction," under-qualified teachers, inadequate laboratories, and the like. She criticized Newark teachers and administrators for failing to properly embrace state-of-the-art classroom techniques. Her book's final chapter enumerated a large number of proposals for positive change in school practice and educational policy, with such sub-titles as: "Renewal of School Leadership," "Preparation of New Teachers," "Programs to Address the Special Needs of Disadvantaged Students," "Full-Service Schools," and "Funding and Educational Reform."[33]

Still, the lion's share of her argument and narrative was dedicated to the proposition that meaningful urban school reform was unlikely to succeed as long as large numbers of inner-city children continued to experience the endemic hopelessness and chaos that results from poverty, racial isolation, and their many effects—problems she had audacity (or mere common sense) to relate to the dialectically inseparable hierarchies of capitalism and racism. These structural inequalities, Anyon felt, bore tragic fruit in the troubled lives of the human "raw material" that Newark's public schools were supposed to refine into productive citizens and workers. To give a felt personal sense of how the difficult total life experience of ghetto-ized children crippled their educational experience, Anyon prefaced her study with the following disturbing passage from her initial field notes in "Marcy School":[34]

> As I enter the room there is a strong smell of urine. The windows are closed, and there is a board over the glass pane in the door. The teacher yells at a child from her desk, "I'm going to get rid of you!" Some children are copying spelling words from the board. Several of them jump up and down out of their seats. Most are not doing the work; many are leaning back in their chairs, chatting or fussing.

The children notice my arrival and look at me expectantly; I greet them and turn to the teacher, commenting on the broken pane of glass in the door. She comes over from her desk and says, "Jonathan put his hand through the window yesterday—his father passed him on the street and wouldn't say hello. Jonathan used to live with him, but since he started living with his mother, the father ignores him."

"These kids have hard lives, don't they," I say. At that, she begins a litany of the troubles of the children in her class: Derrick's father died of AIDS last week; one uncle has already died of AIDS and another is sick. One girl's father stole her money for drugs. On Monday a boy had been brought to school by his mother, who said that the boy had been raped by a male cousin on Thursday, but that "he was over it now." The teacher was trying to get the boy some counseling. Two boys were caught shaving chalk and "snorting" the dust, and "they aren't getting any counseling either." One boy had a puffy eye because his mother got drunk after she got laid off and beat up the kids while they were sleeping; last night he had hit her back, while she was sleeping.

At this point I interrupt the teacher to say, "It's really stuffy in here. Why don't you open a window?" "I can't," she replies, "because I have some children [points to a tiny girl] who likes to jump out of school windows!" The children are totally out of control now, running around the room. One boy is weeping quietly at his desk. She shouts, "Fold your hands!" They ignore her. I realize I must leave so she can get them back in some order, so I say I will see her next week and go out the door. It locks behind me.

This dismal description provides some context for understanding why Harvard education professor Pedro Noguera goes so far as to say the following in the conclusion to his recent book *Big City Schools and the American Dream*:

It will not be possible to improve urban public schools until our society is willing to address the issues and problems confronting the children and families in the communities where schools are located. Even though there are a small number of schools that manage to serve children well despite the harshness of conditions in inner-city neighborhoods, these will continue to be the rare exceptions. Unless concerted action is taken to alleviate the hardships and suffering related to poverty and to spur development that can lead to economic and social stability for communities and families, little change in the character and quality of urban schools in the United States will occur.

"Given the long history of failure in urban public schools," Noguera argues, "this point should be obvious. Yet, despite the track record of failure, we continue to hear slogans from the federal government like 'Leave No Child Behind' without the political will needed to realize this goal." [35]

CHICAGO NONREVELATION

From the Coleman perspective, then, there was no great call for social or educational justice celebration when Chicago Public Schools CEO Arne Duncan announced, in the spring of 2004, that his gigantic school district actually spent more per student in "predominantly black" (70 percent or more African American) schools than in technically "integrated" (at least 15 percent white) schools. According to previously impossible-to-obtain school-level funding data released in March of last year (in support of the CPS' effort to obtain release from its twenty-four-year-old desegregation order), the city spent $5,336 on each child in the black elementary schools and $5,271 per child in the "integrated" schools. The city, the CPS reported, spent $7,712 per student in predominantly black high schools but $6,320 per student in "integrated" high schools.[36]

There are at least four reasons not to see this data as significant proof that anything close to real racial educational equality was beginning to emerge in the Chicago area. First, the leading source of racial school funding inequity in that region, as throughout the nation, takes places between and among hundreds of different schools districts, with disproportionately white suburban communities spending considerably more per student than Chicago and other disproportionately black jurisdictions in the metropolitan area, whatever the color of relatively narrow school funding differences within the city. Second, it is entirely possible that a considerable part of the greater expenditure in predominantly black schools was dedicated to the maintenance and repair of relatively old and out-dated school facilities and equipment, school safety issues, social work counseling, and/or other programs related to extreme poverty in poor minority communities. Third, as we have seen in chapter two, many relevant racial school inequalities reflect disparities that cannot be measured in purely fiscal terms, including differences in pedagogy, curriculum, teacher quality and attitude. Fourth, if Coleman and his many successors are correct, the impact of school disparity (funding or otherwise) is slighter than that of overall socioeconomic difference between and among students and schools in determining unequal educational quality and achievement. The deepest and most significant educational barriers for children like Rayola Carwell are found in the total environment of the urban ghettoes where nearly a majority of black public school children live.

The nation's predominantly black and Hispanic urban schools are packed with children who bring enormous social-class barriers to learning, barriers that few white children must overcome. No matter how good or bad their schools, principals, and teachers, these students deal with an imposing and interconnected array of educational obstacles resulting from poverty and a daunting number of related "extra-school" factors, including high unemployment, high crime, rampant incarceration and felony-marking, poor health, environmental pollution, and stark family fragility.

Consider, for example, at the data presented in Table 4.1, which combines and compares per-student expenditures, race composition, neighborhood poverty and family structure statistics at four Chicago high schools.[37] Two of these schools—Lincoln Park and Lakeview—are technically (by CPS definitions) "integrated" (at least 15 percent white) and two—Simeon and Westinghouse—are almost exclusively African American. It is comforting, perhaps, to think that students in the two black schools are advantaged compared to their integrated counterparts because the former schools spend slightly more per student than the latter. It is likely, however, that the learning cost of higher child poverty, deep poverty, single-parent family and no-parent family rates (to mention just a few of the environmental extra-school community and family factors that matter) in and around the heavily black schools significantly transcends whatever learning benefit might be conferred by the small school funding premium those schools enjoy. The slightly higher per-student expenditures at Westinghouse and Simeon, moreover, could be the result of any number of causes, including greater expenditures of federal poverty dollars, higher security expenditures, and/or higher facility maintenance bills.[38]

SEGREGATING SCHOOL POVERTY

The persistent, indeed, deepening segregation of urban schools by race merits notice as it is also and at the same time the intensified segregation of those schools by poverty. Fully 76 (72 percent) of 107 Chicago public schools that report 97 percent of their students as "low income" (eligible to receive free lunches) are at least 90 percent black. Just one of those schools—*one*—

Table 4.1 Race, School Funding Equity, Community Area, and Socioeconomic Inequity in Four Chicago High Schools

School and Community Area	Percentage White (School)	Percentage Black (School)	Percentage Hispanic (School)	Low Income by School (Free or Reduced Price Lunch)	Spending per Student	Percentage of Population Living at Twice the Poverty Rate (2000)	Percentage of Population in Community Area Living at Less than One-Half the Poverty Level	Percentage of School-Age Children (5–17) in Community Area Living Beneath the Poverty Level
Lincoln Park (Lincoln Park— North Side)	29.6	35.5	19.0	57.6	$5,548	84.9	4.9	9.2
Lakeview (Lakeview— North Side)	17.3	18.6	58.3	83.2	$6,354	82.5	4.2	14.7
Simeon (Chatham— South Side)	0.0	99.9	0.1	97.4	$6,744	63.1	9.3	22.7
Westinghouse (Humboldt Park— New West Side)	0.0	99.6	0.1	92.5	$6,728	42.5	15.0	38.3

Sources: Chicago Public Schools (2004);[39] Consortium on Chicago School Research (2004).[40]

is 15 percent or more white. Of the city's 293 predominantly black schools, fully two-thirds (170) report 90 percent or more of their students as "low-income." By contrast, just eight of the city's 113 technically integrated public schools put 90 percent of their students in that income category.

This strong correlation between student blackness and student poverty is typical across the nation's public schools. As the Harvard Civil Rights Project noted in a 2004 study titled "*Brown* At Fifty: King's Dream or *Plessy*'s Nightmare?," "the vast majority of intensely segregated minority schools face conditions of concentrated poverty. Students in segregated minority schools face conditions that students in segregated white schools rarely face." In the 2001–2002 school year, the Project reported, 43 percent of the nation's public schools were "intensely segregated" either 90 percent white or less than 10 percent white. Eighty-eight percent of the nation's intensely segregated nonwhite schools experienced "concentrated poverty," defined in terms of the necessary provision of free lunches to more than half of their students. Only 15 percent of the intensely segregated white schools exhibited such high poverty. The higher the nonwhite percentage of a school's population, the Project showed (see Table 4.2), the greater its likelihood of dealing with the special educational barriers created by poverty and its effects.[41]

THE EXTRA-SCHOOL BARRIERS BROKEN DOWN

What precisely are the educational barriers that particularly afflict low-income inner-city schools, students, and communities and how do these barriers obstruct equal and effective learning? Numerous health problems that are disproportionately concentrated among minority urban and poor children— vision and hearing impairments, poor dental condition, high blood lead levels, asthma, low birth weight, mother's prenatal

Table 4.2 Race and School Poverty, 2001–2002

Percentage Black and/or Latino in School	Percentage Poor In Schools			
	0–10 Percent	10–25 Percent	25–50 Percnet	50–100 Percent
0–10	24.7	27.6	32.9	14.8
10–20	20.2	27.6	35.4	16.2
20–30	9.5	35.4	40.3	24.8
30–40	5.1	15.9	42.9	36.2
40–50	5.5	9.2	38.2	47.1
50–60	4.2	4.8	30.4	60.7
60–70	4.9	3.8	19.9	71.4
70–80	4.2	2.4	12.0	81.4
80–90	3.8	2.8	8.8	85.4
90–100	4.3	2.0	6.1	87.6

Source: Harvard Civil Rights Project (2004).[42] Table adapted by the author.

smoking and alcohol use, poor nutrition, and lack of access to health care—all tend to pull down children's capacity to learn. Asthma, to take one example, is an especially big problem in Chicago's black community, where nearly one in four children suffers from the disease. As Richard Rothstein notes in his recent thoughtful and Coleman-esque study *Class and Schools* (2004), "asthma keeps children up at night, and, if they do make it to school the next day, they are likely to be drowsy and less attentive." "Low birth-weight babies," Rothstein notes, "have lower IQ scores and are more likely to have learning disabilities."[43]

At the same time, many children of color deal with shocking levels of trauma and even terror resulting from endemic physical and emotional violence in their homes and communities. "A lot of our students come from broken homes," an inner-city Dean of Elementary Students recently told the Chicago school reform magazine *Catalyst*. "Even for the least little thing, [these students] want to…punch each other." A West Side principal told *Catalyst* about "a girl at her school who regularly beat up other students after *witnessing her father being beaten to death* [emphasis added]. 'She is going to keep pounding people,'" the principal observed, "until she has time to tell her story."[44]

During the early 1990s, Pedro Noguera found some telling disparities when he surveyed Bay Area children on their experience with violence. Fully eighteen of twenty-two students he surveyed at west Oakland's inner-city Lowell Middle School reported knowing someone who had been hurt or killed by violence during the last year. Just six of twenty-eight students at Berkeley's middle-class Willard Middle School knew such a person. The large majority of the Lowell students said they, "often worry about being hurt by someone when I am in school" or "at home or in my neighborhood." Only three students felt that way at Willard. While thirteen of twenty-two Lowell students reported having been in a fight in the last month, just four of twenty-eight Willard students had fought during the same period.[45]

The problem of violence among students is exacerbated in Chicago, *Catalyst* reports, by the fact that many inner-city students are recruited and sometimes born into gangs. A West Side principal who requested anonymity told the magazine about a 12-year-old boy at his school who "can get 50 kids together in five minutes. He's done it," the principal reports, referring to a fight that took place outside his school when "the boy insulted a girl, whose brother started a fight to defend her. Within minutes, 50 children attacked the brother on the 12-year-old's orders." The boy's father, it turned out, is a gang member "and the child's authority stems from that affiliation."[46] A middle-aged African American high school teacher from Rayola Carwell's neighborhood tells me that he has to divide his classes between the members of two violently feuding South Side gangs.

Frequent residential mobility makes it common for poor black children (e.g., Rayola) to attend at least three different schools by third grade, and tend to disrupt the classroom experience in inner-city schools. "Teachers with such mobile students," Rothstein notes, "are more likely to review old rather than introduce new material, and are less able to adjust instruction to the individual needs of unfamiliar students." Moving is a frequent experience for poor urban children, thanks in no small part to gentrification and the shortage of affordable housing for poor families, combined with frequent stints of joblessness and endemic family break-up.

Mobility issues aside, Rothestein notes, "middle-class children usually have a quiet place at home, perhaps their own bedroom, to read and do homework. Poor children in more crowded and chaotic living environments find it much more difficult to "escape television, conversation, or siblings."[47]

To make matters worse, poor children are much less likely than their disproportionately white middle- and upper-class counterparts to have been read to and told stories prior to kindergarten. Books are relatively scarce in poor children's homes and those children spend much more time in front of the television. During reading and conversation times in their families, moreover, poor children are much less likely to be asked questions and encouraged to utilize their critical faculties. They are much more likely than middle-class kids to be told to "pay attention without interruptions or to sound words or name letters." They are surrounded by much less discussion and they are rarely encouraged to participate as equals in conversations by parents who tend to instruct their children in "following orders" instead of showing them how to figure out solutions on their own. "When middle-class parents give orders," Rothstein adds, "the parents are more likely to explain why the rules are reasonable. These parents are much more likely than their lower-class counterparts to help their children with homework and to be directly involved with schools' educational and extra-curricular activities." Lower- and working-class children are much more likely than middle- and upper-class children to be reprimanded and shamed and much less likely to be praised in their daily interaction with parents. Thanks to these and a host of related socioeconomic/class disparities in childrearing style and technique, middle- and upper-class children tend to enter school with much wider vocabularies, far greater confidence in their ability to master academic skills, and a much stronger sense of entitlement to the benefits that modern education promises to provide.[48]

STRUCTURE, CULTURE, AND RACIAL DOUBLE STANDARDS

Reasons to Question the Promised Educational Payoff

Affluent and middle-class children experience school with a much greater feeling of confidence that the hard work required for educational success will open doors to good jobs, higher incomes, and professional or other forms of occupational and economic success. All too often, unfortunately, inner-city children's skepticism about the relevance of education's much-ballyhooed "payoff" is tragically justified. To be sure, blacks who perform well academically are much more likely to be well rewarded in the labor market than was the case in the 1960s.[49] Still, blacks continue to be very disproportionately concentrated in economically marginal, de-industrialized neighborhoods and jurisdictions where employment is shockingly scarce and large numbers of adults are visibly jobless for long periods of their lives. In Rayola's Englewood and in various other neighborhoods among Chicago's twenty-two 90-percent-or-more black community areas, for example, the adult employment-population ratio by 2003 had fallen well below 50 percent.

To make matters worse, labor market discrimination continues to play an important role in generating severe black-white economic inequality in the United States. A recent report released by the Legal Assistance Foundation of Metropolitan Chicago (LAFC) and the Chicago Urban League (CUL) presented the results of an eight-month LAFC/CUL project in which matched pairs of equally qualified black and white female individuals (called "testers") applied for real jobs to determine the extent to which employers show greater willingness to hire applicants solely on the basis of race. This investigation or audit showed that covert anti-black racism continues to operate in an important hiring zone. It revealed a smoking gun of *pure racial hiring bias* by presenting the outcomes of an elaborate testing operation that controlled for education, work experience and residence to measure *unadulterated racial discrimination.*

LAFC and CUL researchers conducted seventy-three in-person employment tests for entry-level retail positions throughout the Chicago suburbs. Matched pairs of black and white female testers, with resumes that controlled for soft skills and previous work experience, visited prospective employers to apply for these job openings. Testers recorded the details of the application process including the initial visit, return visits, interviews, phone calls, and job offers.

White job applicants were favored throughout the application process and consequently received more job offers. White applicants received job offers from more than 80 percent of the employers, whereas black applicants received offers less than 70 percent of the time. Not only did white applicants have a 16 percent higher chance of receiving a job offer, the jobs offered to them included more hours of employment per week.

In addition, LAFC researchers conducted 273 mail-resume tests to employers throughout the Chicago Metropolitan Area. Resumes featuring black- and white-sounding names were mailed to prospective employers who had advertised positions. Black applicants received callbacks one-fourth of the time while white applicants received similar calls one-third of the time. White applicants had a 21 percent greater chance of being called back for an interview than their black counterparts.[50]

This finding of anti-black hiring bias is consistent with other and larger employment testing projects. Between July 2001 and May 2002, researchers Marianne Bertrand of the University of Chicago's (UC) School of Business and Sendhil Mullainathan of the Massachusetts Institute of Technology (MIT) sent out over 5,000 resumes testing 1,300 job openings in Boston and Chicago. Using birth records to determine the most prevalent black and white names, they found that resumes with white-sounding names received 50 percent more callbacks than those with black-sounding names. White applicants with better credentials received 30 percent more callbacks than white applicants overall. Improved credentials did not improve the rate of callbacks for black applicants.[51] Rayola's family, it would appear, may well have paid a labor market and, hence, economic price for its chief breadwinner's clearly black-sounding name.

Blaming the Victim

Such research, a small slice of what might be cited on persistent structural or institutional racism in American life, should remind us not to set up too strong a dichotomy between structural (or political-economic explanations) and cultural (or culture-of-poverty) explanations of inner-city educational problems. Much of the ghetto and ghetto-related behavior that conventional white American wisdom places at the explanatory heart of black poverty can be traced to the negative social conditions that predictably emerge when a branded people are savagely concentrated into a relatively small number of hyper-segregated, isolated, and de-industrialized communities. High rates of teen pregnancy, for example, are strongly correlated with inner-city teenage girls' inability to perceive any future middle-class or even working-class career opportunities that might realistically be ruined by early out-of-wedlock pregnancies. The failure to defer gratification is an all-too-predictable response in neighborhoods where good-paying jobs for local residents are close to nonexistent and less than half of the adult population is attached to the labor market. A similar dynamic is certainly at work in relation to the city's excessive black high school dropout rate.

Meanwhile, the stark absence of visible economic opportunity in the city's least vital communities combines with the high profit-premium placed on the narcotics trade by the aggressive criminalization of certain drugs to "incentivize" black involvement in the illegal drug economy and the attendant gangs that fight to control what they can of that economy. These distressing trends are exacerbated by the profoundly alienating nature of ghetto life (certainly a key factor behind inner-city narcotics demand) and the broader consumerist messages pumped into these neighborhoods by the heavily materialist and commercialized mass culture.[52]

Thanks to the black middle class's persistent high relative proximity to concentrated poverty and related distress in highly segregated Chicago, moreover, the negative cultural pull of the ghetto is not restricted to poor and deeply poor black city residents. "For the [black] middle class," an African-American community developer from Chicago's South Side told the *Chicago Tribune* last year, "it's hard to maintain the high lofty goals you have for yourself when this abject poverty is all around you." "Because of their proximity to the poor," the *Tribune* noted, "middle-class blacks are exposed to styles of behavior and habits that emerge from patterns of racial exclusion and concentrated poverty. These characteristics may not allow them to compete in mainstream society with children who accumulate skills readily acquired in more privileged environments." As the esteemed black sociologist William Julius Wilson told the *Tribune*, "The middle-class residents of the South Side are much more likely to be exposed to crime and other manifestations of social dislocation and social problems. All of this works against middle-class black students." Thanks to their special high exposure to concentrated poverty and its cultural (among other) consequences, the black middle class has to work much harder than the white middle class to maintain the social and cultural attributes that feed and sustain educational success and upward economic and occupational mobility.[53]

Relatively affluent Caucasians, it is worth noting, routinely engage in many of the same self-sabotaging behaviors that mainstream U.S. wisdom sees as the basic explanation of black inequality. They do so without experiencing the same degree of terrible socioeconomic and life changing consequences as those visited upon poor blacks as the price for "bad" behaviors, values, and choices. The latter are too often expected to almost magically transcend their harsh circumstances, exercising an inordinate, practically heroic degree of sound personal responsibility just to keep their heads above water. Meanwhile, many whites are structurally and institutionally empowered "to pass Go and collect $200" while exercising a much slighter degree of responsibility and propriety than that required of the disadvantaged people of color whom Bill Cosby called—at an NAACP event commemorating *Brown*'s fiftieth anniversary (which he used as an opportunity to attack impoverished African Americans)—"the lower economic people." At the same time, extreme focus on poor blacks' culpability tends to unduly exonerate more privileged and predominantly white others for engaging in morally problematic behaviors—widely documented anti-black hiring and real estate discrimination, for example—that contribute to persistent black-white inequality. Personal responsibility's contribution to disproportionate black poverty and misery is, it is too often forgotten, multi-racial. It involves white as well black agency in the creation and sustenance of racial hierarchy.[54] Remembering that some are more structurally empowered than others to generate, maintain, and reduce racial disparity, the brilliant African American historian Manning Marable has recently argued that:[55]

We will never uproot racism by pretending that everyone shares an equal and common responsibility for society's patterns of discrimination and inequality. Black partners were never "equal partners" in the construction of slavery, Jim Crow segregation, and ghettoization. We weren't individually or collectively consulted when our criminal-justice system imprisoned one-third of our young men, or when we continue to be burdened with twice the unemployment rate of whites. To be "color blind" in a virulently racist society is to be blind to the history and reality of oppression.

PERSISTENT DOCTRINAL FAITH IN EDUCATION AS THE SOLUTION

The notion that educational policy and practice alone cannot fulfill *Brown's* promise for minority children in inner-city and other segregated, high-poverty schools should hardly be controversial. It is supported by an abundance of social science research and no small measure of elementary common sociological sense. It is a long-established principle of developmental psychology, moreover, that children cannot grow up to be healthy and successful adults unless basic needs—security, nutrition, housing, honoring and recognition of self, etc.—are met.[56]

Nonetheless, the seemingly obvious idea that schools and students require a supportive and democratic environment (societal, emotional, and physical) in which to succeed is sadly beyond the limited parameters of America's official educational policy debate. That debate remains significantly committed at both ends of a narrow spectrum that seems addicted, in the proud American tradition, to the idea that schools are the solution not just to educational problems but, indeed, to broader societal problems like poverty, unemployment, and inequality. In the 2000 presidential campaign, for example, George

W. Bush and Al Gore argued over which educational changes would do the most to eradicate the supposedly small remaining "pockets" of poverty in the United States. Bush favored market-driven reforms like vouchers, private contract schools, and charter schools. Gore wanted to invest more federal dollars in the repair of crumbling schools and the hiring and training of more teachers. The two candidates agreed, however, on the need to impose high test-based standards on failing schools in poverty-concentrated areas and on the notion that schools are the basic answer to economic disadvantage and inequality. The notion of America's strikingly high and heavily racialized inequality of socioeconomic condition was not even remotely included in, or acknowledged as part of, the quadrennial national education pseudo-discussion.

Bush's reactionary No Child Left Behind Act, it is worth recalling, was passed with bi-partisan support in 2001, with critical backing from the Republican's great liberal *bete noir* Senator Edward Kennedy (D-Massachusetts). The NCLB responded to the "achievement gap" by mandating rigorous testing standards for all racial, ethnic, and socioeconomic student groups. Failing schools that do not miraculously shrink racial, ethnic, and socioeconomic test-score differences—standardized test score disparities are actually supposed to disappear by 2014 under the legislation—are threatened with a loss of federal funds. Such schools are supposed, as we have seen, to give their students the right to transfer to higher-performing schools.

Beneath grandiose promises and requirements, however, the NCLB provided little in the way of resources for segregated high-poverty schools to make a serious attempt at meeting the new standards. The White House reneged on an initial promise to spend nearly $6 billion to the help the nation's poorest schools jump through the new "no excuse" testing hoops being held up by the Education Department (part of this sum went to help relieve giant corporations from paying a minimum alternative tax). Meanwhile, Henry Giroux noted in 2003, "One of the most misplaced appropriations in Bush's federal funding for schools has been earmarked for increased testing to provide a measure of teacher accountability—as if teachers can be held responsible for crumbling buildings, the disappearance of school lunch programs, overcrowded classrooms, and a chronic shortage of textbooks, computers, and other necessary educational resources. Similarly," Giroux added, "Bush has been silent about providing substantial increases for federal educational programs such as Title 1, which specifically aid poor and disadvantaged students."[57]

Yet even were such resources forthcoming, more than a little unlikely given Bush's harshly regressive and imperial agenda (see chapter five), the NCLB simply does not address what Peter Irons calls "the serious problem of the 'total environment' of the urban ghetto in which close to half of all black children live." However good their schools and teachers, Irons argues, "black children who come from this environment come to school with obstacles to effective learning that few white children must overcome." Failure to deal seriously with concentrated minority poverty, Irons feels, is the first of "two major drawbacks" in "the proposals to improve American schools that are currently fashionable." The second limit is contemporary American school reform's "reliance on standardized testing to measure results," a dependence that "pressure[s] teachers to rely on old-fashioned methods of rote learning, the mainstay of Jim Crow schools," which "stifle...creativity, curiosity, and critical thinking."[58]

Both of Irons' two concerns were entirely absent from the educational components of the 2004 presidential campaign. The conservative incumbent Bush upheld educational accountability and high standards, touting the NCLB as the embodiment of these principles and criticizing liberals' supposed "bigotry of low expectations." John F. Kerry, who voted for the NCLB, criticized Bush's failure to provided adequate funding to enable poor schools to meet the law's "unfounded [test-score] mandates." In one of the finer moments in his generally lackluster campaign, Kerry won points in civil rights circles by acknowledging that the United States was still violating the spirit of *Brown* decision by maintaining "two [persistently] separate and unequal school systems" and advocating a shift of national resources from the incarceration to the education of black youth.

The negative impacts of the deeper inequality and the standardized test obsession were off the table of serious presidential debate. This even as a long economic slowdown was combining with savagely regressive tax policies and related federal local, state, and federal budget cuts and massive imperial defense expenditures to significantly worsen the material socioeconomic situation of the urban poor, moving the number of black children living in deep poverty from less than 700,000 to more than 1 million between 2001 and early 2003.

Bush took the American political tradition's naïve faith in schools' capacity to overcome social and economic difficulties to an absurd extreme. This is what he had to say during the last of the three presidential debates, when CBS television reporter Bob Schieffer asked the president how he would respond to "someone who has lost his job to someone overseas who is being paid a fraction of what that job paid here in the United States?" [59]

You know, there's a lot of talk about how to keep the economy growing. We talk about fiscal matters. But perhaps the best way to keep jobs here in America and to keep the economy growing is to make sure our education system works. I went to Washington to solve problems. And I saw the problem in the public education system in America. They were just shuffling too many kids through the system, year after year, grade after grade, without learning the basics.

And so we said: let's raise the standards. We're spending some money, but let's raise the standards and measure early and solve problems now, before it's too late.

No, education is how to help the person who's lost a job. Education is how to make sure we've got a workforce that's productive and competitive.

Got four more years, I've got more to do to continue to raise standards and to continue to reward teachers and schools that are working, to emphasize math and science in the classroom.

One wonders how this analysis went over with a parent who had recently been laid off after his or her job was out-sourced to a low-wage section of the world economic system. The children of such ex-workers faced heightened extra-school barriers to learning resulting from their parents' unemployment and Bush's simultaneous slashing of government social services (in the name of personal responsibility) to pay for exorbitant tax cuts for the already super-rich and for expensive, illegal imperial adventures in the Middle East. As Rothstein notes, "When a parent's income falls, or a parent loses a job, there are [negative] educational consequences for children."[60] Low wages, poverty, and unemployment, three widespread consequences of the onetime self-described "education president" Bush's domestic social policies are educational problems for the children of the poor and working classes.

Meanwhile, back in my home city of Chicago, nobody in any position of public influence or responsibility bothers to look beneath the public school system's recently released school-by-school funding data to examine the deeper inequality in and around the city's segregated schools. There is no serious main-stream discussion of the unpleasant fact that the city's ambitious cutting-edge school reform plan particularly targets neighbor-hoods marked for upscale gentrification. If and when high test-scores are posted by the city's reconstituted "Renaissance" schools, city and school officials, their corporate sponsors and beneficiaries will take the credit for the new educational suc-cess, ignoring the ugly detail that the poorest children were pushed out of the relevant local school attendance zones and conveniently forgetting to mention that students of higher so-cioeconomic status score higher primarily for reasons having to do with their more elevated class positions and related more learning-friendly home and neighborhood environments.

The city's two major corporate newspapers continue to print stories about the city's many failed local schools, neglecting, in most cases, to pay more than cursory attention to the severe educational consequences of concentrated poverty and racial segregation. The papers also report that the local principals and school administrators are finding ingenious ways to artificially boost test scores and reduce apparent achievement gaps: delet-ing the scores of students who transfer in late and of those who did not answer all test questions, expelling low-scoring chil-dren with behavior problems, and discouraging transfers in by low-scoring students.[61] At the same time, the city's school chief has unveiled a special "interactive web-site" where the "the public" is encouraged to "provide input" on what precise crite-ria should be used to determine which of the city's hundreds of "chronically low-scoring schools" should be closed down.[62]

Meanwhile, private educational testing design, publication, and assessment corporations reap a massive profit windfall. Writers and activists who question the negative and authoritar-ian impact of the national testing rage on Jim Crow's modern day children are criticized by realistic fiscal equity advocates for diverting attention from, and undercutting, the achievement-gap-based case for fiscal equity. The argument for adequate (though not equal) educational resources for poor children, we are told, benefits from the existing test-based "accountability" system and we should "lay aside" our "whole litany" of concerns with testing and use the constantly reiterated spreadsheets of test-score disparity to make the case for separate but "adequate" schools.[63]

THE FALSE CHARGE OF FATALISM

Those who insist that none except a relatively small number of poor schools can heroically leap above harsh material and social-historical circumstances and fulfill *Brown*'s promise alone are sometimes criticized by school reformers (including both conservatives and liberals) as fatalists and economic determinists who think that there's nothing schools can or should do to reform education. This is unfair. Anyon's book concludes with a long list of proposed school reforms that are put forth as part of a strategy for broad social, including educational, change. Richard Rothstein's book *Class and Schools* is subtitled "Using Social, Economic, *and Educational* Reform to Close the Black-White Achievement Gap" [emphasis added] and includes proposals for numerous educational changes, including a significantly expanded public investment in early childhood learning programs for inner-city students. For Rothstein, the finding that unequal circumstances tend to be replicated and passed on by segregated schools "is *not a reason to throw up [our] hands* [emphasis added]. Rather, along with efforts to improve school practices, educators, like the students they try to prepare should exercise their own rights and responsibilities of citizenship to participate in addressing the inequalities with which children come to school."[64]

This comment reminds me of an interesting formulation that appeared at the end of Jencks' book *Inequality*. This formulation is full of meaning for those who agree with me that moral and ideological transformation of school curriculum and pedagogical practice and philosophy belongs at the heart of meaningful modern-day school reform:[65]

> A successful campaign for reducing economic inequality probably requires two things. First, those with low incomes must cease to accept their condition as inevitable and just. Instead of assuming, like unsuccessful gamblers, that their numbers will eventually come up or that their children's numbers will, they must demand changes in the rules of the game. Second, some of those with high incomes, and especially the children of those with high incomes, must begin to feel ashamed of economic inequality. If these things were to happen, significant institutional change in the machinery of income distribution would become politically feasible.

Encouraging such radical and critical awakening in the hearts and minds of America's still savagely class- and race-divided children is a worthy endeavor indeed for educators who wish to create a just and democratic society in which to situate *and enable* quality schooling for all children. The notion that meaningful, progressive school reform requires democratic transformation is fatalistic only to those who are unable or unwilling to imagine such change as a desirable and/or possible development. For others, this writer included, it is a clarion call to combine school reform with broad social reform, reflecting an at-once idealistic and realistic understanding that there's little point in "trying," as Jean Anyon says, "to clear the air on [only] one side of a city door." Serious school reformers, Rothstein rightly notes, "can't think only about school reforms."[66]

5

WHY SEPARATISM MATTERS

Let us be dissatisfied until America will no longer have a high blood pressure of creeds and an anemia of deeds. Let us be dissatisfied until the tragic walls that separate the outer city of wealth and comfort and the inner city of poverty and despair shall be crushed by the battering ram of the forces of justice. Let us be dissatisfied until those who live on the outskirts of hope are brought into the metropolis of daily security. Let us be dissatisfied until slums are cast into the junk heaps of history, and every family is living in a decent sanitary home. Let us be dissatisfied until the dark yesterdays of segregated schools will be transformed into bright tomorrows of quality, integrated education. Let us be dissatisfied until integration is not seen as a problem but as an opportunity to participate in the beauty of diversity.

—Martin Luther King, Jr., 1967[1]

An outside observer sympathetic to the goal of black equality but unfamiliar with the spatial distribution of social and economic opportunity in modern America might well respond to the abundance of available data and research documenting the nation's strong persistent racial separatism by asking "so what?" Contrary to the Supreme Court's reasoning in *Brown v. Board of Education,* racial separation is not *inherently* a corollary of racial inequality. There is no absolute or inviolable law of social and historical development mandating that African Americans could not thrive while living in separate communities.

We should not assume, moreover, that, in a society free of prejudice and discrimination, African Americans would necessarily choose to live dispersed among whites or that the only suitable or proper residential pattern for blacks is one whereby they are absorbed within a white majority. As the great black scholar and activist W.E.B. DuBois wrote seventy years ago, "There [should be] no objection to colored people living beside colored people if the surroundings and treatment involve no discrimination, if the streets are well lighted, if there is water, sewerage and police protections, and if anybody of any color who wishes, can live in that neighborhood. Never in the world," DuBois counseled, "should our fight be against association with ourselves because by that very token we give up the whole argument that we are worth associating with."[2]

In existing society, however, crucial social and economic opportunities are not distributed evenly across space and community. There's a highly unequal geography of opportunity and condition in the United States. That spatial order and hierarchy of place, maintained largely through the discriminatory operation of real estate markets, is heavily racialized to the detriment of black Americans. As sociologist Douglas S. Massey notes, those markets "are especially important because they distribute much more than a place to live; they also distribute any good or resource that is correlated with where one lives. Housing markets don't just distribute dwellings, they also distribute education, employment, safety, insurance rates, services, and wealth in the form of home equity; they also determine the level of exposure to crime and drugs, and the peer groups that one's children experience. If one group of people is denied full access to urban housing markets because of the color of their skin," Massey argues, "then they are systematically denied full access to the full range of benefits in urban society." [3]

It is a matter of no small significance for racial equality that whites and blacks rarely reside in the same communities. As Thomas Sugrue testified in the early stages of the litigation that led to the *Grutter* ruling, "the questions—where do you live? and who are your neighbors? are not trivial. A person's perspectives on the world, his friends, her group of childhood peers, his networks and job opportunities, her wealth or lack of wealth, his quality of education—all of these are determined to no small extent by where he or she lives." [4]

"Where you live," Sheryl Cashin observes, "largely defines what type of people you will be exposed to on a daily basis and hence how well you relate to different types. It often defines what schools you will go to, what employers you will have access to, and whether you will be exposed to a host of models for success." In Cashin's view, segregated housing "contributes to pervasive inequality in this country and to social gulfs of misunderstanding." [5]

Racial segregation, Lawrence Bobo has noted, is the "structural linchpin of American racial inequality." [6]

It was not for nothing that Martin Luther King, Jr. worried about the spatial division of metropolitan America between inner black cities zones and out white peripheries. "I see nothing in the world," King said in 1967, "more dangerous than Negro cities ringed by white suburbs." [7]

It should come as little surprise, then, that African Americans, with no special desire for white neighbors per se, prefer to live in racially mixed communities and are much less likely than whites to avoid neighborhoods with large numbers of people of races different than their own.[8] To be sure, black Americans give strong and relatively high support for the goal of diversity as such: for the intrinsic democratic value of schools, workplaces, medias, and political structures that accurately reflect the full racial and ethnic heterogeneity of the populace. But "most African-Americans," notes Cashin, "do not crave integration, although they support it. What seems to matter most to us is not living in a well-integrated neighborhood but having the same access to the good things life as everyone else."[9] "My dream," an African American prisoner/student recently told a white prisoner/student in a college history class at an Illinois correctional facility, "is not to sit at the lunch counter next to you. It's just to get the same stuff you order at that counter."[10]

African Americans need hold no particular desire to live near whites to see the benefits of living in an integrated community. They need only to understand from experience that differential access to housing markets tends to generate social stratification by sorting access to educational, commercial, recreational, natural, civic, medical, and labor market opportunity.[11] Many of them, no doubt, also understand the perverse and viciously circular interaction that has developed between poverty and segregation in metropolitan America. Beyond harming the interests of individual black people and households, housing segregation undermines the black community as a whole by concentrating the poverty it helps generate, often at remarkable levels. Concentrated black poverty results from segregation because, Massey notes, "segregation confines any general increase in black poverty to a small number of spatially distinct neighborhoods. Rather than being spread uniformly throughout a metropolitan environment, poor families created by an economic downturn are restricted to a small number of geographically isolated areas." And "since individual socioeconomic failings" tend to "follow from prolonged exposure to concentrated poverty," the whole community tends to be caught in a downward cycle of impoverishment and "everything that is correlated with poverty: crime, drug abuse, welfare abuse, single parenthoods, and educational difficulties."

A toxic, mutually reinforcing relationship of dark reciprocity develops between racial segregation and the experience of poverty's effects. Under conditions of no black segregation, Massey points out, increasing the black poverty rate from 10 to 40 percent would have only "a modest effect on the neighborhood environment that blacks experience." In a highly segregated urban area, by contrast, increasing overall black poverty produces a dramatic (and terrible) impact on that environment. "This sharp increase in neighborhood poverty has a profound effect on the well-being of individual blacks, even those who have not been pushed into poverty themselves, since segregation forces them to live in neighborhoods with many families who are poor."[12]

SCHOOL INTEGRATION: TRIED AND FAILED?

Has integration been tried sufficiently to be demonstrated as either a success or a failure in the education system? It depends on how you use the term. If integration is taken to mean little more than pure and simple desegregation, then it is clear that the United States did undertake a significant experiment in integration, one that developed at a dramatic, even radical pace from the mid-1960s through the early 1970s. This experiment led to at least three documented successes: higher achievement for black students, increased occupational aspirations and status for black students who attended integrated schools, and increased social interaction and tolerance among and between Americans of different racial and ethnic backgrounds.[13]

Unfortunately, American policymakers have been systematically dismantling this democratic experiment since at least the Reagan era. At the same time, desegregation did not move forward without significant costs for the interrelated causes of racial justice and black power. Black Americans experienced the dissolution of many of their own educational institutions and bore the primary travel and time burdens in a mostly one-way (black-to-white) process.

Things look even less positive, however, when we define school integration in Thomas Pettigrew's terms of "genuine acceptance and friendly respect across racial lines." Such true integration would have had to transpire in a reciprocal, two-way fashion, with white children going to formerly black schools as commonly as black children went to formerly white schools. The likelihood of its occurrence would be immeasurably greater if blacks and whites did not stand on profoundly unequal socioeconomic ground outside schools walls. How democratically transformational and racially healing is it, at the end of the day, to move extremely poor and culturally disadvantaged black children from a ghetto community to a white school on the other side of the tracks—a school situated in a community where the black students are not really welcome and cannot afford to live? On top of these children's already considerable pre-existing disadvantage, such integration adds the burdens of an often onerous school commute and the challenge to black students' self-esteem that results from their inability to keep pace, on the whole, with their new, relatively privileged classmates and their numerous educational advantages.

The true school integration that Pettigrew imagined probably requires a measure of social, economic, and political equality between blacks and whites that has yet to remotely emerge in a society where black median household net worth is equivalent to one-tenth of white median household net worth. And since residential segregation by race (when combined with geography-based school attendance zoning) critically generates and reinforces racial socioeconomic disparity as well as apartheid schools, such true integration significantly depends also on the desegregation of American housing markets.

The harsh reality fifty-one years after *Brown* is that this sort of real, profound, and many-sided integration has *not been seriously attempted* in the United States. In fact, the nation seems less likely to try it, as politicians, policymakers, and opinion-shapers embrace neoliberal and neoconservative ideals. Under the rule of these overlapping and often mutually reinforcing ideologies, the meaningful fulfillment of *Brown*'s promise and King's dream is unimaginable. Even the promise of *Plessy* is pushing things.

THE POVERTY OF SCHOOL REFORM

In the absence of official recognition and mainstream acknowledgement that anything could or should be done about educational race-class apartheid in the new white supremacist corporate-neoliberal state, educational equality proponents are supposed to humbly bow before the gods of personal responsibility, standards-based accountability (testing and more testing), and supposed fiscal austerity. The deep school and social inequalities examined in this book are beyond the narrow parameters of acceptable debate in a political culture that takes poverty, classism, racism, separatism, and their multiple, interrelated effects off the table of serious discussion. We are expected to stand mute as political candidates, policymakers, and media authorities rail in socially de-contextualized rage at failing public schools, whose many problems are all-too-predictable with an overall framework of harsh and deepening racial and socioeconomic apartheid. We are instructed to focus on what Pedro Noguera calls "the latest policy gimmick or cure-all—more testing, charter schools, vouchers," as if,

Noguera writes, "there were a silver bullet or special [school-specific] formula that could easily solve the problems and fix the schools"[14] without also repairing the cities and society in which those schools are situated.

"Golden Spike" Fact and Fiction

Education literature in this chilling era bubbles with book, article, school, and program titles and slogans announcing the latest example of a school or educational program that defies the fatalistic bigotry-of-low-expectations crowd by posting high test-scores in poor and segregated schools: "Every Child, Every School," "Stand and Deliver," "Miracle in East Harlem," "The Golden Spike Schools," "The High-Flying Schools," "Success for All," "There Are No Shortcuts," the "90/90/90 Schools" (where 90 percent of the kids are poor, 90 percent are nonwhite, and 90 percent meet state testing standards) and "No Excuses: Lessons From 21 High-Performing, High-Poverty Schools." At the academic heights of reactionary educational wisdom, Abigail and Stephen Thernstrom have recently published a widely read monograph titled *No Excuses: Closing the Racial Gap in Learning*.[15]

When written or conducted by liberals, such allegedly transforming school studies and programs acknowledge that good student outcomes (high test-scores, of course) result in part from the provision of adequate educational resources and that the replication of such successes on a broad scale would require increased public-educational funding, especially where children struggle with concentrated poverty and its common corollary racial isolation. For the rightist Thernstroms, the Heritage Foundation, the American Enterprise Institute and their ilk, however, the secret to minority school achievement has nothing to do with fiscal provision or social reform. For these and other conservatives, it's all about class and racial

grievances—mere excuses of dubious merit aside—and trans-
mitting basic academic skills and traditional Western (whiter
and middle class) values: hard work, persistence, proper respect for authority, good manners, appropriate clothing, and
the like. Rejecting supposedly convenient liberal and left ra-
tionalizations for school failure such as poverty, racism (which
the Thernstroms think has essentially disappeared[16]), and
school funding inadequacy, the heroic leaders and staff of the
educational right's good schools transcend negative surroundings and limited resources by emphasizing the basics, testing
students frequently, instilling discipline, and replacing poor
teachers with more effective classroom performers. In many of
these poverty-be-damned schools that beat the demographic
odds, charismatic, specially skilled, and highly motivated principals and teachers step up to the plate to heroically demolish
the bigotry of low expectations.

Do we have anything to learn or otherwise gain from high-
performing, high-poverty, and high-minority schools? Certainly we do, in many cases, remembering that nobody knows
exactly how much schools can be made to matter relative to the
broader social environment in children's lives. In all likelihood,
the best inner-city educators approach their work *as if* there
was practically no limit to their ability to make up for their students' extra-school disadvantages. Golden-Spike schools, moreover, can provide inspirational and useful evidence to counter
the dangerous notion that minority children are culturally
or, worse, genetically incapable of learning. As recently as the
middle 1990s, it is worth recalling, Charles Murray and Richard Herrensteins' chilling neo-eugenicist "social-science" tract
The Bell Curve made nonfiction bestseller lists with the Social-
Darwinian argument that the racial achievement and earnings gaps reflect differential genetic intelligence endowments.

At the same time, we should guard against biased evidence,
specious reasoning, and deceptive argumentation regarding

what poor and racially segregated minority schools can be expected to attain without significant additional school resources and broader egalitarian social change. Nobody who seriously argues that America's particularly harsh brand of heavily racialized socioeconomic disparity tends to undermine democracy claims that poor people of color *never* achieve *any* policy victories in the United States. No serious Marxist who argues that structural barriers prevent most poor and working-class Americans from becoming rich would deny that an exceptional few such Americans do manage to climb high up the nation's socioeconomic ladder. In a similar vein, nobody who argues that cigarette smoking tends to cause lung cancer can intelligently deny that some people live long and relatively healthy lives while smoking a pack of cigarettes a day. "We understand," Richard Rothstein notes, "that because no cause is rigidly deterministic, some people can smoke, keep handguns, speed, or drink to excess without harm, but we also understand that, on average, these behaviors are dangerous. Yet despite such understanding," Rothstein observes, "quite sophisticated people often proclaim that the success of some poor children proves that poverty and other social disadvantage does not cause low achievement."[17]

In examining the schools that conservatives trumpet as examples that concentrated poverty and racial isolation are merely excuses for school failure, moreover, Rothstein makes some interesting discoveries. He finds that many of these schools are less successful than is generally known on their own standards-based terms. He also reports that many of these schools are much less disadvantaged than their reactionary fans let on. Using the simple standard of subsidized lunch eligibility for identifying poor schools, the Heritage Foundation fails to make a reasonable and appropriate distinction between students from permanently poor and culturally disadvantaged households (e.g., Rayola Carwell) and students from culturally advantaged families whose parents are only temporarily poor while finishing higher-educational degree programs. Heritage's "No Excuses" roster, for example, includes a school that enrolled the children of graduate students at Harvard and MIT and another where 42 percent of the students' parents had bachelor's degrees or more. Another "No Excuses" school was a special "gifted" program reserved for low-income children with unusually high IQ scores. In fact, only six of the twenty-one schools were nonselective neighborhood schools. The remaining fifteen were selective in at least one way, reflecting special admission criteria and curricular offerings that appealed to parents who are specially motivated to choose successful schools for their children. Such children and parents are all too sadly atypical in the inner city.[18]

In one example they provide as a supposedly relevant model for inner-city schools across the nation, the Thernstroms cite the story of Los Angeles' "super-teacher" Rolfe Esquith. Esquith has almost no black pupils. His students are poor but he only teaches children with unusually high IQs and he requires students to stay in class until 6 p.m. He raises considerable extra school dollars from wealthy benefactors to pay for special class activities, including trips to Washington, DC. He also spends massive amounts of unpaid extra time with students, after school and on Saturdays. "When he began teaching," Rothstein notes, Esquith "raised money for books, airfares [for student field trips], musical instruments, and theatrical production by working extra jobs at night and on Sundays, and barely sleeping. He delivered take out meals, worked as a messenger, and ushered at rock concerts to earn extra funds for class activities." This might all be admirable but, as Rothstein notes, it "is no formula" for how large numbers of inner-city teachers might produce good educational outcomes for larger numbers of poor and racially isolated children of color. What Esquith's example shows, rather, "is how expensive are after-school, weekend, and summer activities for children who don't get them at home, and how impossible it is to duplicate the benefits middle-class children receive without finding a way of duplicating similar activities."[19]

Any vision of inner-city educational reform that depends on highly atypical poor kids and heroic teachers (e.g., Esquith) or principals (e.g., Jamie Escalante of "Stand and Deliver" cinema fame) is going to be stuck citing exceptions that prove the rule of inequality and racism's terrible impacts on poor minority children's educational experience. Such supposedly odds-defying stories tend to divert us from the tasks of providing *all* students and schools with the resources they need and introducing the broad social reform—including true, many-sided integration—that would allow poor and racially isolated children to integrate educational excellence into their lives.

Restructuring, Charter Schools, and Small Schools

Miracle schools aside, there is a constant buzz in public educational policy and academic circles about what does and doesn't work inside the nation's urban apartheid schools. One academic analysis of recent organizational innovation's impact inside such schools identifies the following restructured practices in American middle schools during the 1980s and 1990s:

> exploratory classes in academic specialists; special projects developing depth of knowledge of all students; heterogeneous grouping for all academic subjects; high participation in ungrouped academic subjects; cooperative learning techniques in classrooms; shared instruction across grade levels; shared instruction across subject levels; policies discouraging punitive 8th-grade retention; keeping the same classmates for all classes; placing students in smaller schools within schools; giving students the same home-

room teacher or advisor for all middle-school years; common planning time for department members; flexible time scheduling of classes; reduction of department divisions between teachers; staff-development activity directed toward issues concerning young adolescence; team-teaching either between or among departmental members.

The same study gave the following list of restructured practices in American high schools:

parent workshops on adolescent problems; student satisfaction with courses important; strong emphasis on parental involvement; strong emphasis on increasing academic requirements; student evaluation of course content important; outstanding teachers are recognized; emphasis on staff stability; emphasis on staff-development activities; students keep same homeroom over high school; emphasis on staff solving school problems; parents volunteer in the school; interdisciplinary teaching teams; independent study in English/social studies; mixed-ability classes in math/science; cooperative learning focus; student evaluation of teachers important; independent study in math/science; school-within-a-school; teacher teams have common planning time; flexible time for classes.

Which of these restructured practices do the most to foster what the study's authors call "equity and excellence" for poor and minority students? How well do such practices do in overcoming the impact of poverty and racial isolation on "educational outcomes?" I confess to being unable to determine the answers to these questions after reading the highly technical monograph that purports to clarify the issues but does little more than vaguely suggest that such "restructuring" is mildly correlated with test-score gains and enhanced test-score equity.[20]

Are charter schools—public schools run by independent, commonly nonprofit organizations—a good way for urban schools to go toward fulfilling the promise of *Brown*? Definite answers are elusive. A federal Department of Education analysis released in mid-December 2004 found charter students scoring "significantly lower than regular public school students in math, even," the *New York Times* reports, "when the results are broken down for low-income children and those in cities." In reading, we learn, "there was no statistically significant difference between students in charters and in regular public schools. However, when students in special education [mostly absent from charter schools] were excluded, charter students scored significantly lower than those in regular public schools." And when broken down by race, the *Times* reports, the results show charter students "generally lagging behind those in regular public schools, but the differences were not statistically significant." This report confirmed an earlier critical study released by the American Federation of Teachers and using the same statistical data set. Oddly enough, the latest charter school study was described by the pro-charter Bush administration's Education Department as "encouraging" for the charter cause. But charter advocates were reduced to claiming that "charter school students in the aggregate are in a dead heat with students at regular schools."[21]

To make matters worse, there are indications that charter schools work to exacerbate segregation by excluding low-performing students and special-needs children through strategic recruitment, intensely rigorous application processes, and the counseling-out of students who are determined to be "not a good fit." In Boston, one researcher recently reported, charter schools "do not enroll the full range of diverse students that the Boston public schools do."[22]

Is educational downsizing part of the answer for segregated inner-city schools? New York City has signed up to open two hundred new "small schools" by 2008 with financial assistance from the Bill and Melinda Gates Foundation. Chicago (as we have seen) and Los Angeles are also both committed to massive small school experimentation over the next decade. Public educational authorities in these and other urban areas are influenced by early research claiming to show that smaller schools raise test-scores and graduation rates for minority inner-city students. However, distinguished urban education professor Michelle Fine warns that many small schools "just create smaller versions of problematic structures" and other experts worry that standardized testing regimes undercut small schools' ability to deliver on their core promise of a more personalized and individualized education. Numerous school reform proponents warn against a naïve rush to "smallness" as some sort of urban-educational "panacea."[23]

THE VOUCHER DIVERSION: DARK AGENDA AND FALSE SOLUTION

Private School at Public Expense

What about vouchers, the use by parents of public school funds to pay for their children's tuition at often religious private schools? For Bush and other neoliberal and/or neoconservative faith- and market-based school reformers, this is the real and ultimate solution to the cult of public education: the diversion of taxpayer dollars from the transparent common public educational fund to the more authoritarian, unaccountable, and private spheres of market and church. Their project starts, naturally enough, with the race- and poverty-segregated schools of the inner city, whose predominantly black and (understandably) educationally dissatisfied parents and community leaders have been specially targeted by voucher publicists.

Bush was unable to get vouchers encoded in the No Child Left Behind Act. Nonetheless, the NCLB embodies key neoliberal principles by permitting low-income families to use federal funds to transfer their children to better-testing public schools, including charter schools run by private organizations. It provides federal dollars for poorly testing students to receive outside tutoring, which can be gotten from for-profit businesses and religious organizations. "Within this approach," Henry Giroux notes, *"the crucial problem of how the public might provide a better education for all children is narrowly transformed into the issue of how dissatisfied parents can get a better education for their own children* by simply removing them from [their current] schools." [emphasis added] The bill also endorses "punishing failing school districts by turning them over to the state, which in turn can invite for-profit institutions such as Edison Schools, Inc., to manage them—precisely what is currently happening in Philadelphia, the seventh largest school system in the United States." Market-based education reformers know very well, Giroux adds, that charter schools "open the door for the privatization of public education" and "offer various for-profit educational companies a market for significant monetary gain." At the same time, it seems likely that full-scale public school privatization is the real long-term agenda behind the NCLB. The stark disparity between its high test-score requirements and its low level of provision for "failing" schools, many urban school reformers think, is designed to prove the inherent dysfunctionality of public schools and the need to replace them—starting with "poorly performing" inner city schools—with private- and faith-based institutions.[24]

Racist and Rightist Origins

The voucher movement is not new; it dates as far back as the 1950s, when public-to-private school vouchers were used as a tool for white families to escape school desegregation. At the same time, conservatives who were ideologically committed to a free market system of education supported vouchers in the name of school choice. These early voucher advocates influenced conservative political leaders to push for public subsidies to pay for tuition and tuition tax breaks for private school families all through the 1960s and 1970s. During the 1980s, then-President Ronald Reagan consistently spoke in favor of school vouchers.[25]

The adoption of the Milwaukee program in 1990 invigorated the voucher movement and led to the adoption of voucher programs in several cities and states around the country. Large public voucher programs were established in Cleveland and Florida in 1996 and 1999. A number of private voucher scholarship programs sprouted in cities like New York City, Dayton, Ohio, and San Antonio, Texas. Minnesota, Iowa, and Illinois have established tax breaks for families who send their children to private schools. After unsuccessfully attempting to create a federal voucher program, the current White House has established tax breaks for families who use education saving accounts to pay for private school tuition.[26] In early 2004, the Republican Congress approved a White House bill establishing an experimental program permitting at least 1,700 poor District of Columbia students to receive vouchers worth as much as $7,500 to pay for a private school education. The program is projected to cost as much as $200 million by 2009.[27]

The Pro-Voucher Argument

Voucher proponents begin by noting the obvious. They open by repeating the well-known fact that the nation's urban public education systems serving disproportionately black and Hispanic poor students leave their students woefully disadvantaged in the competition for higher degrees and remunerative employment. Vouchers, they claim, permit some inner-city students to escape these failed schools.

Voucher supporters argue that students who receive vouchers experience improved standardized test performance, claiming that black voucher students' scores are higher than black students who applied for but did not receive vouchers. They also claim that the threat of competition from the private sector will improve student achievement for students left behind in the public schools as low-performing public schools upgrade to improve to prevent the loss of students and funding to private schools.[28]

Voucher advocates proclaim that poor parents of color should have the right to choose where their child goes to school. It is unfair and essentially racist, they argue, that poor and minority students are forced to attend poorly performing schools. Vouchers, they insist, open the door of opportunity for these victims of the liberal educational establishment—of what the pro-vouchers black U.S. Supreme Court Justice Clarence Thomas calls the "romanticized" ideal of universal public education. Vouchers, the argument goes, permit some of those children to be "saved" by attaining the chance to attend private schools normally reserved for the disproportionately white middle and upper class.

Voucher proponents also claim that there is strong public support for vouchers, especially in the black community. They cite a 2001 Gallup Poll of 1,108 respondents where 52 percent of public school parents supported voucher programs. A 1999 poll conducted by the Joint Center for Political and Economic Studies, a leading black think-tank, found that the majority of 1,678 respondents favored vouchers. Sixty percent of black respondents, including nearly three-fourths (72 percent) of blacks earning less than $15,000 per year, supported vouchers. A 1999 Public Agenda survey of 1,200 found that 68 percent of black respondents supported vouchers.[29]

The Case Against Vouchers

However, the case for vouchers as a meaningful solution for any but a few of Jim Crow's children collapses under serious scrutiny. Leaving aside the important question of whether or not standardized tests offer a valuable or productive measure of student performance, existing research on privately financed voucher programs shows no consistent pattern of improvement across subject, grade, and length of time. In a comprehensive study of a large-scale private school voucher program in New York City during the 1990s, the leading educational think-tank, Mathematica Policy Research, Inc., found an at-best weak relationship between vouchers and improved school performance for students receiving vouchers. "On standardized tests," Mathematica found, "students offered a scholarship generally performed at about the same level as students in the [non-voucher] control group."[30]

The research on publicly financed voucher programs' performance is also less than encouraging from a standards-based approach. The official research team designated by the Wisconsin state legislature to analyze the Milwaukee voucher program concluded that voucher students performed no differently on standardized tests than did Milwaukee Public School students. Students who received vouchers did no better than those who applied but didn't receive them. Research on the Cleveland voucher program finds that there may have been improvements in science and language, but there was no improvement in other subject areas. And the nonpartisan federal Government Accountability Office (GAO) has concluded that research on the achievement benefits of public voucher programs is "inconclusive."[31]

Vouchers generally provide insufficient funding for poor students to attend private schools. The average voucher, both public and private, in 2001 was worth between $1,500 and $2,000.[32] Private school tuition, especially at the high school level, generally costs considerably more (elite big city private schools cost as much as $15,000 to $20,000 a year and up) than that. The low dollar value of most existing vouchers prevents poor students from attending most private schools.

Parents' right to choose under the voucher option is further limited by the fact that private schools rigidly control admissions to limit the pool of eligible students who use vouchers. Beyond the lotteries that are used to narrow the pool of public school students eligible for vouchers in every public program except Florida's, private K–12 educational institutions can and do turn away students with learning disabilities, limited English, or behavioral problems. In Florida, 93 percent of the private schools will not accept students with vouchers. Some Milwaukee schools have turned away all students with vouchers, while others have turned away students based on ability, gender, and religion.[33]

At the same time, some private schools make parental involvement and other special investments of time and effort a prerequisite to admission. The typical inner-city single mother who works one or more jobs, often with a considerable commute, cannot meet such requirements.[34] Only students with quality private schools in their community are in geographical position to benefit from voucher programs. The poorest urban communities, not to mention virtually all rural areas, have little spatial proximity to such schools.

Of course, the threat of market-based competition worsens the pedagogical problem of "teaching to the test" in public schools. It also heightens those schools' incentive to remove low-performing students from official test-score tabulations by expelling them or classifying them as "special" students: "limited-English," "bilingual," "special education," or "learning-disabled."

Ironically enough, however, there is little standards-based accountability in voucher programs. Private schools are not required to test students, release test data, provide services for special education or learning-disabled students, and even to hire certified teachers. Milwaukee dropped the requirement to monitor the achievement of voucher students in 1995. And private schools are not required to respect constitutional protections such as free speech, due process, or equal protection, and do not have to obey laws prohibiting discrimination on the basis of sex, sexual orientation, marital status, or pregnancy.[35]

School vouchers would have less resonance and relevance in current education policy debates, of course, if the public school system was structured so that all students receive adequate and equitable school resources simply by virtue of their status as citizens-to-be in a democratic commonwealth. Like so much of the public sector activity that the American right and its business-class sponsors label as "tax and spend" liberalism and even "socialism," the actually existing public school system in America works in no small part to preserve and expand private privilege. Beyond deflecting attention from public schools' needs, desegregation issues, and the broader structural and socioeconomic situation, voucher programs divert actual funds from the public educational sector, thereby exacerbating the very public school crisis that gives so much false progressive legitimacy to the voucher movement in the first place.

Real and meaningful school choice, voucher critics rightly note, exists only when everyone has reasonably good options from which to choose. It doesn't exist when parents and students must select between a good choice and a bad one and/or when their access to good choices is harshly limited by the interrelated lotteries—both real and figurative—of class, race, and place. All schools, including public schools, should be adequately funded institutions with high quality teachers and state-of-the art equipment and facilities.[36]

Sensing the basic justice of this conclusion, perhaps, voters have rejected every one of the eight statewide voucher referendums that have reached state ballots since the 1970s. Since 1972, the highest vote percentage received by a pro-voucher referendum is 36 percent—this in spite of the fact the voucher proponents have spent significantly more money than voucher opponents to advertise their position.[37]

As these results suggest, public support for vouchers is much shakier than voucher proponents let on. The Joint Center's 1999 poll found that 63 percent of the general public, 66 percent of school parents, and 60 percent of voucher supporters know "very little" about vouchers. When queried about their understanding of this school "reform," 80 percent of the general public, 81 percent of parents, and 75 percent of voucher supporters reported that they "need to learn more" to have an intelligent opinion.[38] Polling questions on vouchers, it should be noted, tend to be devoid of context and plagued by abstraction. If the polls were properly constructed to gauge true popular sentiment on vouchers, respondents would be asked if they would support school vouchers over equitably funded and truly integrated schools with small class sizes and well-trained, highly motivated teachers. The majority of respondents would certainly say "no" to such a question. In fact, polling data suggests a great deal more support for increasing and equalizing school spending and desegregating schools than for vouchers.[39]

As Cashin notes, "the school voucher movement...delays or deters us from dealing with the inevitable, underlying issues of inequality." Voucher experiments, she argues, "hold out the promise for a relatively few disadvantaged students to escape low-performing schools, but they do not hold any hope of ever doing the same for all children. It would be too expensive and neither the infrastructure nor the money is there to absorb every disadvantaged child into better-performing private or public schools. In fact," Cashin adds, the voucher strategy "ensures that this will never happen because it avoids the hard work of building consensus for that necessary course. We need," Cashin concludes, "to frontally address how we can bring about a transformative integration—a quality middle-class educational experience—for all students rather than focus on the red herring of giving just a few children this option." [40]

It is also worth noting that publicly funded vouchers to attend religious private schools conflict with the separation of church and state mandated by the United States Constitution. Fully 85 percent of private schools in the nation are religious. After removing private schools that are so academically selective and expensive that vouchers don't apply, the percentage is even higher. Government programs that fund religious schools even by mere default (reflecting the absence of nonreligious schools in many locales) violate the First Amendment. Public funding, either direct (a government check to the school) or indirect (a government check to the parents), for religious schools is in fact unconstitutional. As Supreme Court Justice David Souter noted in his dissent to a 2002 Court decision supporting Cleveland's voucher program:[41]

> In the city of Cleveland the overwhelming proportion of large appropriations for voucher money must be spent on religious schools if it is to be spent at all. The money will thus pay for eligible students' instruction not only in secular subjects but in religion as well, in schools that can fairly be characterized as founded to teach religious doctrine and to imbue teaching in all subjects with a religious dimension. Public tax money will pay at a systemic level for teaching the covenant with Israel and Mosaic law in Jewish schools, the primacy of the Apostle Peter and the Papacy in Catholic schools, the truth of reformed Christianity in Protestant schools, and the revelation of the Prophet in Muslim schools, to speak only of major religious groupings in the republic.

LOOKING FORWARD:
THE REVITALIZATION OF *BROWN'S* DREAM

What is to be done to fulfill the promise of *Brown*—equal educational opportunity for all children, including poor children of color? The provision of meaningful high quality school options for *all children*, not just a privileged and fortunate few, means broad-based, systemic education reform, including the following attributes listed by Amy Gutman in an article titled "What Does School 'Choice' Mean?":

> decreasing class size, setting high standards for all students, engaging students in cooperative learning exercises, empowering principals and teachers to innovate, increasing social services offered to students and their families, and providing incentives to the ablest college students to enter the teaching profession and, in articular, to teach in inner-city schools. [42]

In pursuing this meaningful advancement of educational choice for *all* the children of segregation, we should not pretend that inner-city communities of color possess the resources, or for that matter, the responsibility to solve their education problems and fix their schools entirely on their own. There are reasons to find hope in and lessons from the often heroic efforts of independent black schools that have done well in an oppressive context that fails to provide poor, segregated schools and communities the full set of resources and opportunities they need and deserve. But there is little practical point or justice in making a virtue out of self-help necessity and letting state and society off the hook of deep responsibility for the creation and repair of the special educational disadvantages produced by the living legacy of segregated schooling. As economic development continues to move yet further away from and against the nation's ghetto residents, there is no basis for thinking that marginalized inner-city neighborhoods possess the social capital to independently extend significant quality education to their children.[43] At the same time, a notion of educational reform that depends on the inordinate, super-heroic efforts of exceptional education professionals—superintendents, principals, and teachers—is not likely to yield significant educational progress for any but a small number of modern racial apartheid's schools.[44]

The significantly corporate-driven high-stakes testing regime that has been nationally enshrined in the NCLB should be significantly rolled back. The mind- and soul-deadening neo-Dickensian testing craze is imposed with especially harsh authoritarian emphasis and consequence on segregated inner-city schools. It attacks creativity, critical thinking, and democratic pedagogy and suppresses moral and intellectual aspiration. It drives good teachers away from schools that most need skilled classroom personnel and places impossible (as well as distorted) achievement demands on the nation's poor and isolated minority schools. It is pointless and morally suspect to expect students, teachers, and principals in such schools to start posting high test-scores in short order—as if people who run an occasional 12-minute mile could be expected to match up competitively in a long-distance running race with seasoned marathoners. This expectation is so ridiculous, especially when it is not accompanied by significantly expanded school resources, as to make serious analysts question its sincerity. I am neither the first nor the last observer to suspect that the real agenda behind the false reform of high-stakes testing and the NCLB is to advance the hard-right school privatization project by setting goals that the public educational system cannot possibly meet in the absence of revolutionary social change that is anathema to U.S. policymakers.

It is fantasy to expect that free market forces will bring the educational reform and improvement that segregated minority students need and deserve. Vouchers have an understandable if somewhat superficial and qualified appeal to many black parents, whose children are stuck at the bottom of the not-so public school system's privilege-preserving hierarchy. But schools, not parents, retain the real choice over who is admitted to what private schools under voucher systems and the supply of good private schools with the ability and incentive to provide quality educations for poor children of color is strictly limited. Vouchers will not get any but a fortunate few such children into the most truly high-performing schools within a private educational sector that is every bit as (if not more) unequally structured as the public system. Further, there is no reliable evidence that relatively unaccountable and secretive private schools out-perform public schools in educating low-income students of color.

The supposedly liberating forces of the capitalist free market, it is worth noting, have rarely worked to the advantage of any but a relative minority of African Americans. Why and how such forces could be expected to operate on behalf of the most disadvantaged members black community in the delicate and difficult work of cultivating young hearts and minds is something of a mystery.

Along the path to revitalizing *Brown's* promise, there is no point in denying that providing quality education for all poor minority children will require the allotment of significant additional public-financial resources. There is no cost-free way to provide expanded social services, highly rewarded and well-trained teachers, improved school materials, and small class sizes (to list just a small number of the most urgently needed school changes) to the nation's millions of disadvantaged students.

At the same time, it should be frankly acknowledged, *schools cannot do it alone.* No combination of improved (to use Roy Brooks' terminology) educational "hardware" (school-funding dollars) and "software" (educational programming/restructuring) is going to miraculously boost inner-city schools above their harsh material and social-historical circumstances and simply negate the many interrelated extra-school disadvantages that so powerfully burden children at the bottom-rung intersections of racism, capitalism, corporate globalization, and metropolitan sprawl.

At the end of its 2003 report on race and class school-funding disparities, the liberal Education Trust intelligently links organizational or instructional school reform to education funding reform. Unless the educational programming software is refined in such a way that heightened educational taxpayer expenditures can be shown to "pay off," the Trust argues, it is difficult to make the case for increasing the public school-funding. Bearing in mind many educational researchers' findings on the strong impact of the deeper inequality on children's educational experience, shouldn't serious school funding reformers also make the same argument about the interdependence of educational finance reform and social reform? Unless we improve social conditions—working to clean the air outside as well as inside the school screen door, to use Anyon's analogy—in a way that permits poor minority children to benefit from quality education, then it's hard to make the case for investing more taxpayer dollars in the provision of such an education to an inner-city child.

Who is the *fatalist* here? Is it the activist who builds on this interdependence to call for broad simultaneous and mutually reinforcing educational and social transformation? Or is it the one who concludes that the deeper inequality is a permanent, immutable reality and that meaningful change is only possible within the important but limited and immediate sphere of education?

The broader reform that is required, which will also not come cheap, must involve considerable specific attention to racial as well as class and socioeconomic problems. African Americans continue to face numerous racially specific barriers to equality—obstacles that simply cannot be reduced to blacks' class-based socioeconomic disadvantage or the tragic economic legacy of past racism. These barriers include widely documented racial discrimination in U.S. labor, real estate, and financial markets as well as in the criminal justice, health care, media, and educational systems. Bearing in mind that black

Americans' deep comparative socioeconomic disadvantage is critically rooted in persistent residential race apartheid, moreover, we should note that the broader social reform required for the realization of *Brown's* promise must include a serious effort to break up the ghetto and attack the nation's segregated housing markets.[45]

Imperial Garrison-State Priorities

The richest and most powerful national on earth, the United States, does not even remotely lack the necessary material and financial resources to make good on *Brown's* promise through a dramatically escalated and simultaneous investment in both educational and social reform. We do not have to look far to determine where we might find the assets to properly serve children victimized by social and educational class and race apartheid in the post-civil rights era. As of 11:15 p.m. on December 21, 2004, the National Priorities Project (NPP) reported, the George "No Child Left Behind" Bush administration's imperial war of choice in Iraq had cost more than $151 billion. With that same sum of money, the NPP calculated, the United States could have: enrolled 20,037,391 U.S. children in Head Start for one year; provided health insurance for one year to 90,588,264 children, built 1,362,157 public housing units, *and* hired 2,621,749 additional public school teachers for one year. In Illinois, where Rayola Carwell attends a ghetto school where class sizes are too big to permit individual attention to students, the state's share of the war's cost could have paid for the construction of 772 new elementary schools. The City of Chicago's share could have paid for the hiring of 27,284 additional teachers for one year.[46]

Meanwhile, federal funding for education fell far short of need. In 2004, NPP reported, Title 1 programs to improve teaching and learning for disproportionately minority "at-risk" (poor) children fell more than $7 million short of need. Federal allotments to Improve Teacher Quality fell $245 short and funding for the nation's "21st Century Community Learning Centers" (for disadvantaged students and their families) fell $1 billion short.[47]

Such shortfalls are hardly surprising when we consider that the military eats up 29 cents of every federal tax dollar, compared to just 4 cents spent for education.[48] They seem even more predictable when we learn that the total costs of the Bush administration's harshly regressive tax cuts had reached $297 billion by 2004, equivalent to 2.6 percent of the national Gross Domestic Product. These cuts put government revenues at their "lowest level as a share of the economy since 1950" and contribute "to the dramatic shift from large projected budget surpluses as far as the eye can see," the mainstream Center for Budget and Policy Priorities (CBPP) reports. By CBPP's calculations, just 8.9 percent of Bush's supposed "middle-class tax-cuts" went to the middle 20 percent of American income earning households. The wealthiest 1 percent received 24 percent of the cuts. Each such household would have received an average tax reduction of $34,992. Millionaire households, equivalent to 0.2 percent of all U.S. households, received 19.3 percent of the tax cuts by 2004. These households received an average tax reduction of $123,592.[49]

The average beginning teacher salary in the United States in 2003 was $29,564. In Rayola's state, the average such salary was $34,522,[50] just $470 less than the average tax cut enjoyed by the top 1 percent in what was already the industrialized world's most unequal and wealth-top-heavy nation by far before Bush came into office.

Things don't look much better for federal funding for inner-city schools and communities in 2005. In a front-page Christmas season *Wall Street Journal* article titled "Sharpening the Knife: Bush Vows to Halve Deficit, Targets Already Feel

Squeezed," reporter Jackie Calmes noted that concerns about the spectacular scale of the U.S. deficit meant less money for education among other areas of public investment that ranked far below the radically regressive and repressive Bush administration's primary commitments to empire and inequality. New Hampshire Republican Senator Judd Gregg, the new Chairman of the U.S. Senate Budget Committee proclaimed that first Congressional session of 2005 "cannot afford to be a guns and butter term. You've got to cut the butter."

"With guns—or military spending growing," Calmes explained, "the butter" to be cut was "likely to include some of the most visible areas of domestic spending, including the Medicaid health program, subsidies to Amtrak, agricultural research, and even some federal education programs." It didn't help that Bush "had ruled out raising taxes and is widely expected to win an extension of his first-term income and corporate tax-cuts, moves that will reduce revenue flowing into the Treasury beyond his presidency. Moreover," Calmes added, "both Mr. Bush and Congress are committed to changing the alternative minimum tax (AMI), a levy designed to prevent rich taxpayers avoiding taxes altogether." And "fixing [that is abolishing] the AMI," Calmes observed, "will cut projected tax revenues by hundreds of billions of dollars." In seeking to cut revenues to pay for imperial war and regressive tax cuts, Calmes wrote, "about 85 percent" of the federal budget "is almost untouchable by public consensus." The "remaining discretionary funds— and the areas Mr. Bush has targeted for shrinking"—included "breast cancer research, *aid to rural and inner-city schools* [emphasis added], veterans' medical care, weather forecasting, and park rangers." Poignantly enough, Calmes noted that the amount of money paid by the federal government for interest on its national debt—$168 billion in annual payments, "much of it to overseas holders of Treasury bonds"—is "more than the government will spend on education, housing, transportation, science, space, and technology combined."[51]

Turning to the state and local levels, policymakers looking for resources to pay for adequately and equitably funded schools could examine exploding incarceration budgets. Between 1980 and 2000, state and local mass imprisonment expenditures rose from a total nationwide cost of $6.4 billion to $51 billion (in inflation-adjusted dollars) as the nation embarked on a massive prison-construction boom to warehouse almost one million prisoners at the turn of the millennium. Nearly half the people behind bars in the world's leading incarceration state are African American and most of the nation's massive army of black prisoners and ex-prisoners are the products of the nation's highly disadvantaged apartheid communities and schools. By 2000, the Justice Policy Institute (JPI) reported in a study titled "Cell Blocks or Classrooms?," there were "nearly a third more African American men incarcerated than in higher education" in the United States. Roughly half the giant U.S. prison and jail population has not completed high school or received a GED and black high school dropouts are especially over-represented among the one-in-three African American male adults who lived under one form of supervision (prison, probation or parole) by the criminal justice system by the mid-1990s.[52]

The Myth of the Powerless, Cash-Strapped State

According to a common lament, progressive change in America is impossible because of the powerless and cash-strapped state. American government can't really do anything anymore, this complaint says, because it doesn't have the strength, the legitimacy, the money, and the wherewithal to carry out key objectives. The national policymaking elite's supposed ideological preference for free markets, the story goes, has hopelessly disabled the state's capacity to serve those at the bottom of the nation's multiple, intersecting hierarchies of race, class, gender, age, status, and power.

The lament is broken down as myth when we appreciate the corporate-connected privileged class's persistent reliance on state protection and public subsidy and when we ask *whose* objectives American government *can* and supposedly *can't* carry out. In the wealthiest nation on earth, the public sector lacks the money to properly fund education for all of the country's children. It lacks the resources to provide universal health coverage, leaving forty-two million American without basic medical insurance. It can't match unemployment benefits to the numbers out of work. It lacks or claims to lack the money to provide meaningful rehabilitation and reentry services for its many millions of very disproportionately black prisoners and ex-prisoners, marked for life with a criminal record. The list of unmet civic and social needs goes on and on.

It is interesting, however, to learn what our public sector *can* supposedly pay for. It can afford to spend trillions on tax cuts rewarding the top 1 percent in the thoroughly disingenuous name of "economic stimulus." It can spend more on the military than on all of America's possible "enemy" states combined many times over, providing massive subsidy to the high-tech corporate sector, including billions on weapons and defense systems that bear no meaningful relations to any real threat faced by the American people. It can afford hundreds of billions and perhaps more than a trillion dollars for an invasion and occupation of distant devastated nation that posed minimal risk to the United States and even to its own neighbors. And of course, it can afford to incapacitate and incarcerate a greater share of its population than any nation in history and to spend hundreds of millions each year on various forms of corporate welfare and other routine public subsidies to private industry. "It will be a good day," as the venerable peacenik bumper sticker says, "when the Pentagon has to hold a bake sale to pay for its next B-52 bomber."

The American public sector, in short, is weak and cash-strapped when it comes to social democracy for the people but its cup runs over in powerful ways when it comes to meeting the needs of wealth, racial disparity, and empire. Free market discipline is reserved primarily for children and families of the poor, who just happen to be disproportionately nonwhite.

It's useful to keep these distinctions in mind when we hear people like the powerful Republican tax cut maven and political strategist Grover Norquist say that their goal "is to cut government in half in twenty-five years, to get it down to the size where we can drown it in the bathtub." When Norquist and his followers say they want to "starve the beast" of government, they target some parts of "government" for malnourishment a lot more energetically than others. They are most concerned with dismantling the parts of the public sector that serve the social and democratic needs of the nonaffluent majority of the American populace. They want to de-fund what the late French sociologist Pierre Bordieu referred to as "the left hand of the state," the programs and services that embody the victories won by past popular struggles and social movements for justice and equality. They want to reserve the right hand of the state, the part that provides service and welfare to the privileged few and doles out market discipline and direct public punishment to the poor, from the budgetary axe.

Their wishes are being met. Under the pressure of an imperial "war on terror" and a relentless, well-funded political and ideological campaign led in its most extreme forms by radically regressive Republicans like Norquist, Newt Gingrich, and Karl Rove, the public sector offers rich benefits to the privileged few even as the state is being stripped of its social and democratic functions. State policy toward the disproportionately disadvantaged black population is increasingly reduced to policing and repressive functions, which are expanding in ways that are more than merely coincidental to the assault on social supports and programs. The corporate state increasingly criminalizes and thereby deepens social inequality and related social problems through self-fulfilling prophecies of racially disparate (racist) mass surveillance, arrest, and incarceration, the home-land counterpart to the racially disparate hyper-militarization of regressive global U.S. empire.[53]

Toward a Pedagogy of Hope and Liberation and "The Production of Free Human Beings"

The main obstacles to the fulfillment of *Brown*'s promise of educational equality for the victims of contemporary educational apartheid are moral and ideological. They are found in the widespread dissemination and acceptance of the notion that racism is no longer a significant barrier for blacks and that the only remaining obstacles to black success and equality are found within the African American community itself. They are found also in the related, broadly hegemonic ideas that economic inequality and social hierarchy are right, natural, and/or inevitable facts of life and that there is nothing that the populace and/or government can or should do to establish control over the great tyrannical private-economic institutions that impose savage social hierarchy life and regressive/repressive policy in the United States.

They are traceable in part to the neoliberal, corporate-imposed erosion of the social-democratic public spaces that once served as the forums in which communities and peoples debated, analyzed, and participated in political life. Indeed, we have witnessed in recent decades an unprecedented decline in popular engagement, the process by which common people asserted their interests and took responsibility for their common destiny. The result has been the privatization (consumerization) of American life, with its concomitant sense that social action and responsibility are futile propositions, stillborn by their very nature. There is a broad, deep, skeptical, even cynical sense that nothing much can be done about existing social problems—"The Wheel in the Sky Keeps on turning"—and that the only reasonable solutions to societal difficulties are to be found in private realms, matters of purely personal correction. The world has grown too complex—too ossified—to be subject to meaningful collective agency. This sense masks despair as "realism" and retreat from democracy and social responsibility as mature personal "adjustment."[54]

To see one way this fatalism is disseminated throughout American society, we might turn, curiously enough, to the state lottery systems that purport to help finance public schools. In the mainstream literature on primary and secondary education, these systems hold relevance primarily as flawed school funding instruments, as regressive revenue mechanisms that help state governments create the illusion that they are providing significant direct and additional dollars to underprivileged schools. As sociologist David Nibert has shown, however, the lotteries and their advertisements are also loaded with rich and reactionary ideological meaning for the poor and minority people who make up a disproportionately high share of those who play the legalized modern-day version of what used to be called "the numbers game." The lotteries that have spread across the United States since the 1970s play a dark ideological and—one might add, following Henry Giroux—*pedagogical* role in legitimizing inequality among the residents of poor and working class communities. They "teach" a number of false and reactionary lessons, claiming to show that:[55]

- Great wealth is a matter of pure chance, not a product of structural inequality.
- "Anyone can play" and "anyone can win" in the "level playing field" that is the American "land of opportunity."
- Acquiring great purely individual wealth is the central purpose of human experience and the best thing that could ever happen to someone.

- People don't need to join together and fight collectively for social and economic justice and political equality but should focus instead on purely individual activities and advancement.
- The best response to inequality and alienation in the workplace is not to organize with your fellow workers for a more equitable democratic and meaningful work experience, but rather to escape the workplace and leave your fellow workers behind by acquiring a fortune.
- Individual status and wealth are largely matters of pure chance that can be altered, however, through superstition: "play your lucky number."

Of course, the lottery commercials and billboards are just one part of a broad cultural, ideological, and pedagogical order that works to manufacture mass consent to social and political hierarchy. Among the many conservative ideas and teachings that recur again and again in America's corporate-crafted mass entertainment, commercial, and self-help popular culture are the notions that individual effort is superior to group solidarity, that supposedly free enterprise American (state) capitalism is the best possible economic system, and that societal ills are the product of individual malfeasance rather than of underlying structural forces. Equally ubiquitous in our popular (actually corporate) culture are the ideas that human beings are inherently competitive and prone to seek individual gain over social good, that upper middle-class professionals and businesspeople are more interesting and worthy than blue-collar and service workers and poor, and the U.S. foreign and military policies are directed toward democratic ideals and are a necessary civilizing and defensive force against foreign savagery, backwardness, and aggression. American entertainment media and evening news shows regularly advance the idea that law enforcement needs and deserves a freer hand in its contest with a mass of crazed and disproportionately nonwhite criminals. The media mocks people who protest existing social hierarchies as deluded neurotics (if not lunatics) and portrays labor unions as corrupt, antidemocratic institutions that working people would do best to avoid.

Leading capitalist media has, since the 1960s, curiously aligned itself with and profited from counter-cultural rebellion against the corporate state and religious conservatives. This corporate "conquest of cool" (left business and cultural historian Thomas Frank's excellent phrase) is displayed in clever advertisements in which anarchic youth undertake "hip" resistance to "square" authority figures and puritanical ideals by purchasing supposedly liberating products (from Nike shoes to the latest software) and services (online stock trading) provided, ironically enough, by repressive and authoritarian corporations. As Robert Cirino put it more than twenty years ago, "we're being more than entertained."[56]

The vital task of countering these and other powerful reactionary messages is, among other things, pedagogical work. It involves telling students openly and honestly about the harsh facts of social, including educational, hierarchy in modern America. It also calls for educators to help students develop a critical framework in which to comprehend and propose egalitarian and democratic alternatives to the "savage inequalities" of American "life." It requires a vision of a just and democratic future and a realistic belief that desirable alternatives to the current dispensation can be constructed and sustained. Diametrically opposed to the current craze for authoritarian "grill and drill" instruction, it calls for something that is very much within the sphere of schools' capacity—the development of a radical "pedagogy of hope" (Paulo Freire's phrase), democracy, equality, and liberation and the abandonment of the current dominant pedagogy of oppression, inequality, hierarchy, and fatalism. [57]

Such a pedagogy would equip students to understand and act against the broad conditions of inequality that challenge their educational experience within and beyond school walls. Promising something more radical and inspiring than just the provision of a sound and basic education that is merely adequate for the competent docile and passive execution of servile tasks at or near the bottom of the authoritarian corporate state, it would be about what the great American educational philosopher John Dewey considered the highest true purpose of liberal U.S. institutions, including especially the public schools: "the production" not of commodities but "of free human beings." Believing that workers should be "the masters of their own industrial fate" and not simply the hired tools of their more "highly educated" class and cultural "superiors," Dewey considered it "illiberal" and "immoral" to train children to work "not freely and intelligently but for the wage earned." The point of worthwhile schools, Dewey believed, was to cultivate critically engaged citizens capable of actively participating in a true, many-sided democracy, the practice of which meant confronting the unpleasant fact that "politics is the shadow cast on society by big business."

It is a sorry testament to the power of authoritarian nationalism in post-civil rights America that calling for such libertarian values in U.S. classrooms "sounds," in Noam Chomsky's words, "exotic and extreme, perhaps even anti-American." As Chomsky noted eleven years ago in Chicago, the notion that education ought to be public and about radical, many-sided democracy is "as American as apple pie" and firmly rooted in the classic liberal Enlightenment ideals in whose name this nation was founded.[58]

Notes

INTRODUCTION

1. Ellis Cose, "*Brown v. Board:* A Dream Deferred," *Newsweek* (May 17, 2004).

2. Samuel G. Freedman, "Still Separate, Still Unequal," *New York Times* (May 16, 2004).

3. For my own previously published take on modern racism and its different levels, see Paul L. Street, "A Lott Missing: Rituals of Purification and Deep Racism Denial," *The Black Commentator* (December 22, 2002), at http://www.blackcommentator.com and http://www.nationinstitute.org/tomdispatch/index.mhtml?pid=258; "'How You Gonna Export Something You Ain't Even Got At Home?' Notes from Chicago'," Black Commentator (April 26, 2003), at http://www.blackcommentator.com; Paul Street, *Still Separate, Unequal: Race, Place, Poverty, and the State of Black Chicago* (Chicago: The Chicago Urban League, March 2005).

4. Henry A. Giroux, *The Abandoned Generation: Democracy Beyond the Culture of Fear* (New York: Palgrave-MacMillan, 2003), 1–70; Henry A. Giroux, *The Terror of Neoliberalism: Authoritarianism and the Eclipse of Democracy* (Boulder, CO: Paradigm Publishers, 2004), 1–53.

5. Peter Irons, *Jim Crow's Children: The Broken Promises of the Brown Decision* (New York: Penguin, 2002), 344.

6. Jonathan Kozol, "Educational Apartheid Fifty Years After *Brown*," Keynote Address at Chicago Urban League Conference on the Lessons and Legacy of the *Brown v. Board* Decision," Chicago Historical Society, Chicago, IL, May 10, 2004.

CHAPTER 1

1. Associated Press, "Private Schools Driving De Facto Segregation," *Herald-Tribune.com* (March 16, 2003), retrieved July 31, 2003 from http://www.newscoast.com.

2. Karla Scoon Reid, "Color Bind," *Education Week* (February 18, 2004), 44.

3. Orfield and Eaton, "Back to Segregation," *The Nation* (March 3, 2003).

4. Chicago Urban League, Department of Research and Planning, "Chicago Public Schools Race, Poverty, and Community Area (2003) Data Set," compiled by The Chicago Urban League Research and Planning Department with assistance from the Chicago Consortium on Chicago School Research, (August 2004).

5. These numbers are consistent with my experience during visits to Chicago's affluent Dearborn Park condominium development during the late 1980s and early 1990s. Built during the late 1970s, Dearborn Park is a partially integrated, majority-white collection of mostly owner-occupied townhouses and apartments located to the immediate south of the city's famous downtown district (known as "the Loop"). When it first went up, the development's mostly professional, upper-middle class residents thought they had been promised a local elementary school districted for only their own children. After considerable protest and activism, however, an economically disadvantaged and educationally underserved black community to the south of Dearborn Park won entrance to the South Loop Elementary School, located in the new development. When I visited my mother, a Dearborn Park resident, during the 1980s, younger parents I met at local playgrounds with my young son routinely told me they would be "leaving for the suburbs" soon. They would escape before their toddler-age children would have to attend school with "those kids from the projects." To this day, there is a noticeable shortage of children in Dearborn Park. On the day of the aforementioned conference, a scene full in its own small way of

significance for the lessons and legacy of *Brown* was re-enacted in Dearborn Park. Buses arriving from impoverished public housing projects south of the development dropped off hundreds of black elementary school students to begin their day at a more than 90 percent black school surrounded by affluent white homeowners. A block or so away, a small handful of white Dearborn Park children waited for smaller buses to take them to some of the city's elite private schools—Francis Parker, the University of Chicago Laboratory School, or the Latin School. A related but reversed scene takes place in some leading Chicago private Catholic Schools each school-day morning. Buses and cars filled with of white children drop students off at prestigious local Catholic high schools like Leo, Mt. Carmel, and DeLassalle. The neighborhoods that provide the home for these schools were once predominantly white working and middle class and have since become majority African American. Their student bodies remain majority Caucasian, but now the students are certain not to stay in or around the neighborhoods in which their schools are situated.

6. Leonard Steinhorn and Barbara Diggs-Brown, *By the Color of Our Skin: The Illusions of Integration and the Reality of Race* (New York: Plume, 2000), 43.

7. Gail Robinson, "New York Schools: Fifty Years After *Brown*," *Gotham Gazette* (May 17, 2004), available online at http://www.gothamgazete.com/article/20040517/200/981. Emphasis added.

8. Lewis Mumford Center for Comparative Urban and Regional Research, *Metropolitan Racial and Ethnic Change – Census 2000,* available online at http://www.mumford1.dyndns.org/cen 2000/ WholePop/WPSegdata/ 1600msa.htm.

9. Gary Orfield, Erica Frankenburg, and Chungmei Lee, "A Multiracial Society With Segregated Schools: Are We Losing the Dream?" (Cambridge: the Harvard Civil Rights Project, January 16, 2003).

10. Charles Clotfelter, *After Brown: The Rise and Retreat of School Desegregation* (Princeton, NJ: Princeton University Press, 2004), 56.

11. U.S. Department of Education, National Center for Education Statistics, Common Core Data, 2001.

12. Steinhorn and Diggs-Brown, *By the Color of Our Skin*, 13; Gary Orfield and Chungmei Lee, "*Brown* At 50: King's Dream or *Plessy's* Nightmare?" (Cambridge: Harvard Civil Rights Project, January 2004); Clotfelter, *After Brown*, 57–74.

13. Steinhorn and Diggs-Brown, 13. "Wilkinsburg, Pennsylvania is 53

percent black," the authors note, "but its schools are 97 percent black. Oklahoma City is 16 percent black but its schools are about 40 percent black."

14. Associated Press, "Private Schools Driving De Facto Segregation," Herald-Tribune.com (March 16, 2003), retrieved July 31, 2003 from http://www.newscoast.com.

15. Steinhorn and Diggs-Brown, 43–44.

16. Clotfelter, *After Brown*, 129–147. Intra-school segregation plays a much slighter role than inter-school segregation in contributing to overall school segregation at the elementary level. This simply "reflects the greater racial disparities between elementary schools, caused by the larger number of elementary schools and their tendency to reflect racially separate residential patterns. High schools, usually larger and serving larger geographical areas than elementary schools, tend to be more uniform in racial composition within each district." See Clotfelter, 134.

17. Clotfelter, 145.

18. Clotfelter, 56; Orfield and Lee, "*Brown* at 50," 20.

19. Clotfelter, 56.

20. David Roediger, *The Wages of Whiteness: Race and the Making of the American Working Class* (New York: Verso, 1991), 12–13.

21. Derrick Bell, *Silent Covenants: Brown v. Board and the Unfulfilled Hopes for Racial Reform* (New York: Oxford University Press, 2004), 97–102.

22. Irons, *Jim Crow's Children*, 189–191.

23. Clotfelter, 7–8, 17–22, 25–27, 31–32, 46–47.

24. Clotfelter, 185.

25. Clotfelter, 13–30, 56.

26. Clotfelter, 26, 27, 56.

27. Gary Orfield and Susan Eaton, *Dismantling Desegregation: The Quiet Reversal of Brown v. Board of Education* (New York: New Press, 1996), 3.

28. Orfield and Eaton, *Dismantling Desegregation*, 19.

29. Clotfelter, *After Brown*, 26–27, 31–32.

30. The 1850 decision is quoted in Bell, *Silent Covenants*, 88–89 and Irons, *Jim Crow's Children*, 14–15. According to Irons, "Jim Crow schooling actually began in Massachusetts in 1820, and spread to other northern and western states during the 1860s and 1870s."

31. Orfield and Lee, "*Brown* at 50," 20.

32. Orfield and Lee, 20.

33. Cose, "*Brown v. Board:* A Dream Deferred."

34. Reid, "Color Bind," 44–46.

35. *Grutter v. Bollinger* (02-242), 288 F.3d 732, available online at http://www.spct.law.cornell.edu/supct/html/02-241.Z0.html.

36. Orfield and Eaton, "Back to Segregation," *The Nation* (March 3, 2003).

37. Diane Rado, Darnell Little, and Grace Aduroja, "Still Separate and Unequal: Most of Illinois' Students Remain in Segregated, Inferior Schools," *Chicago Tribune* (May 9, 2004), sec.1, p.1.

38. Lewis Mumford Center for Comparative Urban and Regional Research, *School Segregation, 1990–2000*, (http://www.mumford.albany.edu/census/index.asp); Sheryl Cashin, *The Failures of Integration: How Race and Class Are Undermining the American Dream* (New York: Public Affairs, 2004), 7–11, 32–38, 319–21; Steinhorn and Diggs-Brown, *By the Color of Our Skin*, 37–38, 91, 97–99, 111; Paul Street, *Still Separate, Unequal: Race, Place, Policy and the State of Black Chicago* (Chicago: The Chicago Urban League, 2005), 107–111.

39. Irons, *Jim Crow's Children,* 203–207, 237–46; Orfield and Eaton, *Dismantling Desegregation*, 9–13, 19, 96, 147, 293, 296, 302, 314–315, 323, 344, 349.

40. Irons, 246.

41. Martin Luther King, speech at Ohio Northern University (1967), available online at http://www.onu.edu/library/onuhistory.king/king.htm.

42. Orfield and Eaton, *Dismantling Desegregation*, xxii–xxiii; Bell, *Silent Covenants*, 126.

43. Orfield and Eaton, xxiii; Bell, 126.

44. Henry Giroux and Susan Searls Giroux, *Take Back Higher Education: Race, Youth, and the Crisis of Democracy in the Post Civil Rights Era* (New York: Palgrave MacMillan, 2004), 197.

45. Bell, *Silent Covenants*, 66.

46. Howard Schuman et al., *Racial Attitudes in America: Trends and Interpretations*, 2nd ed. (Cambridge: Harvard University Press, 1998); Street, *Still Separate*, 2–3, 106–110; Steinhorn and Diggs-Brown, *By the Color of Our Skin*, 6–11, 14–15, 17, 90, 193–196; Douglas S. Massey, "American Apartheid: Housing Segregation and Persistent Urban Poverty," (DeKalb, IL: Social Science Research Institute, Northern Illinois University, 1994).

47. Richard Morin, "Misperceptions Cloud Whites' View of Blacks," *Washington Post*, July 11, 2001, A1.

48. Steinhorn and Diggs-Brown, *By the Color Of Our Skin*, 6–7; Howard Schuman et al., *Racial Attitudes in America* (Cambridge: Harvard University Press, 1998); John McWhorter, *Losing The Race: Self Sabotage in Black America* (NY: Free Press, 2000). A (thankfully) less politically acceptable and more rarely heard argument against the notion that racism maintains that African Americans continue to lag behind whites and other groups in terms of wealth, income, occupational and educational success due to genetic differences between the races in terms of innate intelligence. This was the core argument of a chilling widely read monograph produced in 1994 by neo-eugenicists Richard Herrenstein and Charles Murray—*The Bell Curve: Intelligence and Class Structure in American Life* (New York: Free Press, 1994). On Gates, see Paul Street, "Skipping Past Structural Racism: Center Trumps Left in Recent PBS Series in Race in America," *Black Commentator* (April 8, 2004), available online at http://www. blackcommentator.com/85/85_think_street.html.

49. Derrick Bell, *Silent Covenants: Brown v. Board of Education and the Unfulfilled Hopes for Racial Reform* (New York: Oxford University Press, 2004), 77–78.

50. Cashin, *The Failures of Integration*, xi–xii.

51. Steinhorn and Diggs-Brown, *By the Color*, 7; Stanley Aronowitz, "Race: the Continental Divide," *The Nation* (March 12, 2001); "A Lott Missing: Rituals of Purification and Deep Racism Denial," *The Black Commentator* available at http://www.blackcommentator.com and http://www. nationinstitute.org/ tomdispatch/index.mhtml?pid=258.

52. Martin Luther King, Jr., "A Testament of Hope," 321–322 in Martin Luther King, Jr., *A Testament of Hope: The Essential Writings and Speeches of Martin Luther King, Jr.*, ed. by James M. Washington (San Francisco: Harper Collins, 1986).

53. Godfrey Hodgson, *America in Our Time* (New York: Vintage, 1976), 67–98.

54. Eric Hobsbawm, *The Age of Extremes: A History of the World, 1914–1991* (New York: Pantheon, 1994), 284.

55. Susan George, "A Short History of Neoliberalism: Twenty Years of Elite Economics and Emerging Opportunities for Structural Change," *Conference on Economic Sovereignty in a Globalizing World* (March 24–26, 1999). For an excellent discussion of the origins and hypocrisy of neoliberal doctrine (which reserves state protection and subsidy for concentrated economic power an applies market

discipline only to the nonaffluent), see Noam Chomsky, *Profits Over People: Neoliberalism and Global Order* (New York: Seven Stories Press, 1999), 65–120.

56. Henry A. Giroux, *The Terror of Neoliberalism: Authoritarianism and the Eclipse of Democracy* (Boulder, CO: Paradigm Publishers, 2004), xiii, xiv, xviii.

57. See Paul Street, *Empire and Inequality: America and the World Since 9/11* (Boulder, CO: Paradigm Publishers, 2004); Giroux, *The Terror of Neoliberalism*; Paul Street and Henry Giroux, "Shredding the Social Contract," *ZNet Magazine* (September 4, 2003), available online at http://www.zmag.org/content/showarticle.cfm?ItemID=4133&SectionID=11.

58. Ellis Cose, *Beyond Brown: The Final Battle for Excellence in Education* (New York: The Rockefeller Foundation, 2004), 14.

59. Rado et al., "Still Separate and Unequal."

60. Bell, *Silent Covenants*, 20–28, 160–179. Bell even writes up an alternative, neo-*Plessy*-ite *Brown* ruling, based on what he felt was an appropriately realistic assessment of white resistance to racial integration and the need for black children to attain education equity and effective schooling with a permanently racist and segregated society.

61. Charles Ogletree. *All Deliberate Speed: Reflections on the First Half-Century of Brown V. Board of Education* (New York: W.W. Norton, 2004), 14, 78, 259–293, 311. See also Roy L. Brooks, Integration or Separation? A Strategy for Racial Equality (Cambridge: Harvard University Press, 1996). Brooks shares Bell and Ogletree's concern for educational equity and effective schooling within a persistent and durable context of educational separatism.

62. Cose, "*Brown v. Board.*"

63. Sheryl Cashin, *The Failures of Integration: How Race and Class Are Undermining the American Dream* (New York: Public Affairs, 2004). At the Chicago conference I mentioned at the beginning of this chapter, it was left to white speakers and scholars (principally Gary Orfield and Jonathan Kozol) to speak in positive terms about the accomplishments of school integration and *Brown*. The African-Americans who spoke were distinctly unimpressed with the accomplishments and legacy of the watershed 1954 decision.

64. W.E.B. Dubois, "Does the Negro Need Separate Schools?," *Journal of Negro Education*, volume 4 (1935), 328.

65. A common misperception that Michael Eric Dyson refutes in I *May*

Not Get There With You: The True Martin Luther King, Jr. (New York: Touchstone, 2000), 101–122.

66. King is quoted in Freedman, "Still Separate, Still Unequal."

67. Hodgson, *America in Our Time*, 450.

CHAPTER 2

1 Jeffrey Henig et al., *The Color of School Reform* (Princeton, NJ: Princeton University Press, 1999), 3.

2. Jonathan Kozol, *Ordinary Resurrections: Children in the Years of Hope* (New York: Perennial, 2000), 44.

3. Stan Karp, "Money, Schools, and Justice," *Rethinking Schools* (Fall 2003),

4. Quoted in Donald Moore, Executive Director, Designs for Change, "Crisis: An Alarming Percentage of Hispanic Youth in the Chicago Metro Area Are Dropouts and Jobless," (Chicago: Designs for Change, October 2003), available online at http://www.designsforchange.org/pubs.html.

5. Mary Johnson, "American Schooling Has Failed Children of Color," *Teaching to Change LA*, volume 14, no. 1-3 (2003-04), available online at http://www.tcla.gseis.ucla.edu/equalterms/features/ askput/johnson.html.

6. Chicago Urban League and Voices for Illinois Children, *Illinois School Funding Attitudes: Focus Group Transcripts* (Chicago: Chicago Urban League and Voices for Illinois Children, 2004).

7. Chicago Urban League and Voices for Illinois Children, *Illinois School Funding Attitudes*.

8. Rado et al., "Still Separate and Unequal."

9. Kevin Carey, *The Funding Gap: Low-Income and Minority Students Still Receive Fewer Dollars in Many States* (Washington DC: The Education Trust, 2003), 5–9, available online at http://www2.edtrust. org/ EdTrust/ Product+ Catalog/special+reports.htm#2003); *Education Week*, "Illinois Report Card, 2003" http://www.edweek.org/ sreports/qc04/ state. cfm?slug=17il.h23nts).

10. Illinois Governor Rod Blagojevich, "The State of the State," January 15, 2004, available online at http://www.deva.illinois.gov/gov/includes/contentsossspeech2004.cfm. Emphasis added.

11. Phil Kadner, "Governor Isn't Talking About the Other 54 Cents," *Daily Southtown*, available online at http://www.dailysouthtown.com/ southtown/columns/kadner/x04-pkd1.htm.

12. Glenn McGee, "Closing Illinois' Achievement Gap: Lessons From the 'Golden Spike' High Poverty High Performing Schools," available online at http://www.p20.niu.edu/P20/spotlightschools/ resources. shtml).

13. Human Relations Foundation and Hull House, *Minding the Gap: An Assessment of Racial Disparity in Chicago – Education*, 2003 available online at http://www.hullhouse.org/gap/pdfs. mindingthegap.education.pdf); Street, *Still Separate, Unequal*, 26–106; Paul Street, *The Vicious Circle: Race, Prison, Jobs and Community in Chicago, Illinois, and the Nation* (Chicago: The Chicago Urban League, 2002).

14. Irons, *Jim Crow's Children*, 33, 51.

15. Brooks, *Integration or Separation?*, 19.

16. Irons, 34, 36–37.

17. Brooks, 9–10.

18. Irons, 61.

19. Brooks, 10–16; Irons, 62–79, 129–143, 163.

20. Rachel Moran, "*Brown's* Legacy: The Evolution of Educational Equity," paper delivered at Chicago Urban League Conference on the Lessons and Legacy of Brown v. Board, Chicago Historical Society, Chicago, Illinois, May 10, 2004, 6–7; Peter Schrag, *Final Test: The Battle For Adequacy in America's Schools* (New York: New Press, 2003), 2, 76.

21. Orfield and Eaton, *Dismantling Desegregation*, 144–147.

22. Karp. "Money, Schools, and Justice."

23. Illinois State Board of Education, School District Finance Data for FY 2003, available online at http://www.isbe.state.il.us/sfms/afr.htm; *US Census 2000, SF-1 Redistricting Data*; Paul Street, *Still Separate, Unequal: Race, Place, Poverty and the State of Black Chicago* (Chicago: Chicago Urban League, 2005).

24. Kozol, *Ordinary Resurrections*, 44–45.

25. Kozol, comments in forum assessing the lessons and legacy of *Brown v. Board of Education* titled "Beyond Black, White, and *Brown*," The Nation (May 3, 2004), p.23; Campaign for Fiscal Equity, "New York City Schools Need $5.63 Billion More in Operating Aid and $9.2 Billion for Facilities to Provide a Sound Basic Education, Special Master Panel Recommends," Press Release, November 30, 2004, available online at http://www.cfequity.org/.

26. Kozol, *Ordinary Resurrections: Children in the Years of Hope* (New York: Crown, 2000), 46.

27. Pedro Noguera, *Big City Schools and the American Dream* (New York: Teacher's College Press, 2003), 217.

28. Cose, *Beyond Brown*, 17–18.

29. Cose, 23–24.

30. Peter Schrag, *Final Test: The Battle For Adequacy in America's Schools* (New York: New Pres, 2003), 16–17, 23–24.

31. Schrag, *Final Test*, 56.

32. Schrag, 16–22.

33. Mary Johnson, "American Schooling Has Failed Children of Color," *Teaching to Change LA*, volume 14, no. 1-3 (2003–04), available online at http://www.tcla.gseis. ucla.edu/equalterms/features/ask-put/johnson.html.

34. Jeffrey MacDonald, "Contrarian Finding," *Christian Science Monitor* (December 6, 2004).

35. Chicago Sun Times, "Failing Teachers" (2001), available online at http://www.suntimes.com; Schrag, 32–33, 56, 58.

36. Jeffrey Henig et al., *The Color of School Reform* (Princeton, NJ: Princeton University Press, 1999), 3.

37. Henry S. Giroux and Susan Searls Giroux, *Take Back Higher Education: Race, Youth, and the Crisis of Democracy* (New York, NY: Palgrave MacMillan, 2004), 196.

38. Noguera, *Big City Schools*, 104–105.

39. A.A. Akom, "Racial Profiling at School: the Politics of Race and Discipline at Berkeley High," in William A. Ayers. Bernadine Dohrn, and Rick Ayers, *Zero Tolerance* (New York: New Press, 2001), 53, 61.

40. Brooks, *Integration or Separation?*, 29–30.

41. Kozol, comments in "Beyond Black, White, and *Brown*;" Kozol, "Educational Apartheid Fifty Years After *Brown*," Keynote Address at Chicago Urban League Conference on the Lessons and Legacy of the *Brown v. Board* Decision," Chicago Historical Society, Chicago IL, May 10, 2004.

42. Henry A. Giroux, *The Abandoned Generation: Democracy Beyond the Culture of Fear* (New York: Palgrave, 2003), 75–76, 79, 82–90, 98 (quotation is from 86–87). See also Alfie Kohn, "Standardized Testing and Its Victims," *Education Week* (September 17, 2004).

43. Paulo Freire, *The Pedagogy of the Oppressed* (New York: Continuum, 1997 [1970]), 53.

44. Kozol, comments in "Beyond Black, White, and *Brown*."

45. Asa Hillard, III, comments in "Beyond Black, White, and *Brown*."

46. See Schrag, *Final Test*, 110.

47. Donald Moore, Executive Director, Designs for Change, "Crisis: An Alarming Percentage of Hispanic Youth in the Chicago Metro Area Are Dropouts and Jobless," (Chicago: Designs for Change, October 2003), available online at http://www.designsforchange.org/pubs.html. See Elaine Allensworth, *Ending Social Promotion: Dropout Rates in Chicago After Implementation of the Eight-Grade Promotion Gate* (Chicago: Consortium on Chicago School Research, May 2004), 4–6, 25.

48. Human Relations Foundation and Hull House, *Minding the Gap*, p. 18. See also Rebecca Gordon, Libero Della Piana, and Terry Keleher, "Zero Tolerance: a Basic Racial Report Card," 170–171 in William Ayers, Bernadine Dohrn, and Rick Ayers, *Zero Tolerance: Resisting the Drive for Punishment in Our Schools* (New York: New Press, 2001).

49. Gary Orfield, Daniel Loson, Johana Wald, and Christopher D. Swanson, *Losing Our Future: How Minority Children Are Being Left Behind by the Graduation Rate Crisis* (Cambridge: Harvard Civil Rights Project, 2003), 87–88.

50. Bruce Western et al., "Black Economic Progress in the Era of Mass Imprisonment," 165–180 in Marc Mauer and Meda Chesney-Lind, eds., *Invisible Punishment: The Collateral Consequences of Mass Imprisonment* (New York: New Press, 2003).

51. Steinhorn and Diggs-Brown, 47.

52. Brooks, *Integration or Separation?*, 26; Steinhorn and Diggs-Brown, *By the Color of Our Skin*, p. 47; Clotfelter, *After Brown,* 126–146.

53. ACORN New York City chapter, *Secret Apartheid I* (New York: ACORN, 1996); *Secret Apartheid II* (1997).

54. Carey, *The Funding Gap*, 9–10; Schrag, *Final Test,* 62-63, 66, 71, 74–77, 236, 243.

55. Human Relations Foundation and Hull House, *Minding the Gap,* 21.

56. Chicago Metropolis 2020, *2002 Metropolitan Index,*36–37, available online at http://www.chicagometropolis2020.org/o2_edu.pdf.

57. Karp, "Money, Schools, and Justice." On racial wealth disparities, see Thomas M. Shapiro and Jessica L. Kenty-Dane, "The Racial Wealth Gap," in Cecilia Conrad et al., *Readings in Black Political Economy* (Dubuque, IA: Kendall-Hunt Publishing Co., 2004). It doesn't help the cause of minority educational equality, Karp observes, that blacks are much less likely to vote in local elections that often include budget referenda for public schools, whose students tends to be disproportionately nonwhite.

58. Kozol, in "Beyond Black, White, and *Brown*."
59. Hillard, in "Beyond Black, White, and *Brown*."

CHAPTER 3

1. Quoted in David McCullough, *John Adams* (New York: Simon and Schuster, 2001, 103).
2. Schrag, *Final Test*, 230.
3. Bell, *Silent Covenants*, 161.
4. Bell, 163; Rachel Moran, "*Brown*'s Legacy," 10.; Schrag, 1–3.
5. Campaign for Fiscal Equity, "In Wake of Panel's Recommendation, CFE Vows to Continue Push for Statewide Reform," Campaign for Fiscal Equity (New York: CFE), December 1, 2004, available online at http://www.cfequity.org/.
6. Campaign for Fiscal Equity, "Kansas Supreme Court Gives Legislature Three Months to Make Its Funding System Constitutional," January 4, 2005, available online at http://www.cfequity.org/.
7. Karp, "Money, Schools, and Justice."
8. Karp, "Money, Schools, and Justice." In some states, of course, reactionary courts have ruled against equity lawsuits. In highly regressive Illinois, fiscal-equity advocates believe that state-constitutional language does not permit meaningful legal strategies and they pursue school funding reform only through legislation seeking a trade-off between property taxes and income and sales taxes.
9. Bell, 163–164.
10. Karp. "Money, Schools, and Justice."
11. Moran, "*Brown*'s Legacy," 12.
12. Greg Winter, "At Frontline of School Reform, Progress is Constant But Slow," *New York Times* (December 6, 2004, A1).
13. Cose, *Beyond Brown*, 32, quoting Schrag, *Final Test*, 79.
14. Carey, *The Funding Gap*, 14.
15. Moran, "*Brown*'s Legacy," 13. The Illinois Governor's "State of the State" speech that I excerpted in chapter two is an excellent example of supposed "efficiency" concerns eclipsing the issue of equity: Blagojevich was so obsessed with his definition of educational efficiency (percentage of educational dollars going to classroom instruction) that he was incapable of mentioning, or unwilling to mention, the state's remarkable school funding inequalities (first in the nation!) in a long-winded rant dedicated to the cause of systemic reform in the financing of Illinois public schools.
16. Moran. "*Brown*'s Legacy," 13–21.
17. Schrag, *Final Test*, 230; *Abbot v. Burke*, 119 N.J. 287 (1990), 368.

18. Paul Street, "Comments on School Funding and the Achievement Gap," Education Summit, Roberto Clement High School, February 21, 2004.

CHAPTER 4

1. Jean Anyon, *Ghetto Schooling: A Political Economy of Urban Educational Reform* (New York: Teachers College Press, 1997), 168.
2. Quoted in Stephanie Simon, "Schools a $2 Billion Study in Failure," *Los Angeles Times,* May 18, 2001.
3. Henig et al., *The Color of School Reform* ,3.
4. Richard Rothstein, *Class and Schools: Using Social, Economic, and Educational Reform to Close the Black-White Achievement Gap* (Washington, DC: Economic Policy Institute, 2004), 9.
5. George W. Bush, comments during Presidential Debate, October 13, 2004, available online at http://www.debates.org/pages/trans20od.html.
6. Stephanie Banchero, "One Girl's Struggle," *Chicago Tribune*, July 18, 2004, sec. 1, p.1; "Falling Back," 19 July, 2004, sec.1, p.1; "Starting Over," July 20, 2004, sec.1, p.1.
7. Economic Policy Institute, "Basic Budget Calculator," available online at http://www.epinet.org/ cgioutput.cfm? template=epibudcalc.DJa777&title=Basic%20Family%20Budget%20Calculator.
8. Street, *Still Separate, Unequal.*
9. Combining key statistics from Chicago's twenty-two predominantly African American (90% or more black) neighborhoods, treating them as a collective "city within a city" and comparing this hyper-black inner-city with the overall city and metropolitan areas, leads to some suggestive findings: the collective unemployment rate of the predominantly black twenty-two is nearly twice that of the city as a whole; one-fourth of the children in this predominantly black city within a city—home to three-fourths of the city's African Americans—live in deep poverty; the official unemployment rate of these twenty-two neighborhoods is nearly twice that of the city as a whole. The poverty rate in these neighborhoods is more than three times higher than that of the metropolitan area as a whole. Street, *Still Separate, Unequal.*
10. The Boston Consulting Group, An Analysis of Economic Development and Funds Flow in Chicago (2003).
11. De Paul University political science student Ralph Edwards, "Field-Trip Reflections on Chicago Neighborhoods (May 2004).
12. Street, *Still Separate, Unequal.*

13. Banchero, "One Girl's Struggle."
14. Banchero, "One Girl's Struggle;" Banchero, "Falling Back;" Street, *Still Separate, Unequal.* On Chicago as a "global city," see Charles Madigan, ed., *Global Chicago* (Chicago: University of Illinois, 2004).
15. Banchero, "Staring Over."
16. Amanda Paulson, "Chicago Hope: Maybe *This* Will Work," *Christian Science Monitor* (21 September, 2004), available online at http://www.csmonitor.com/2004/0921/plls01-legn.html. I heard a bit about the plan in advance from an interesting source in February 2004: a young white professional woman enrolled in a graduate-level class I was teaching on race and urban political economy in Chicago. This student worked in "community relations" for one of the city's major banking institutions and had attended a number of meetings where her employer advised the CPS on its forthcoming school reform extravaganza. Meanwhile veteran black school principals on the city's south and west sides had no idea what the city was planning. Many of them learned their own schools were targeted for closure only on the day in June when "Renaissance 2010" was formally announced. My student, a twenty-something white urban professional from the city's affluent North Side, knew more about what was coming around the corner in Chicago's black schools than numerous senior black education professionals.
17. Brooks, *Separation or Integration?*, 30.
18. Kate Grossman, "Tough to Get to Into New School That Meets Standards," *Chicago Sun Times*, November 16, 2004, 18.
19. Amanda Paulson, "In Failing Schools, How Real is Transfer Option?," *Christian Science Monitor* (May 19, 2004).
20. Banchero, "Starting Over."
21. Paulson, "In Failing Schools;" Carey, *The Funding Gap*, 15–16.
22. James Coleman et al., *Equality of Educational Opportunity* (Washington, DC: Government Printing Office, 1966).
23. Hodgson, *America in Our Time*, 446.
24. Henig et al., *The Color of School Reform*, 3.
25. Coleman, *Equality*, 21–22, 290–330.
26. Chicago Public Schools, School Funding Database (March 2004).
27. Christopher Jencks et al., *Inequality: A Reassessment of The Effect of Family and Schooling* (New York: Basic, 1972), 265.
28. Jencks et al., *Inequality*, 253–258; Jencks, *The Academic Revolution* (Garden City, NY: Doubleday, 1968), 111.
29. Brooks, *Integration or Separation?*, 217.

30. Simon, "Schools a $2 Billion Study in Failure;" Alison Morantz, "Money and Choice in Kansas City," in Orfield and Eaton, *Dismantling Desegregation*, 241.

31. Simon, "Schools a $2 Billion Study in Failure."

32. James Traub, "What No School Can Do," *New York Times Magazine*, January 16, 2000.

33. Anyon, *Ghetto Schooling,* xiii–xvi, 3–13, 41–186.

34. Anyon, *Ghetto Schooling,* xii–xiv.

35. Noguera, *City Schools*, 142.

36. Lori Olszewski and Darnell Little, "School Spending Disparity Revealed," *Chicago Tribune* (March 2, 2004); Rosalind Rossi, "Judge Say It May Be time to End Desegregation Deal," *Chicago Sun Times* (March 2, 2004).

37. Consortium on Chicago School Research, "Selected Indicators From the US Census and Chicago Public Schools Records Related to the Lives and Schooling of Children" (Chicago: CCSR, 2004), available online at http://www.consortium-chicago.org/Schoolageenvironment/index.html.

38. Part of the black schools' funding premium likely results from the influx of special supplemental state and federal poverty dollars. It is possible, moreover, that that much of the premium is spent not on direct instruction but on the maintenance and repair of relatively ancient and decrepit school facilities, special safety expenditures and/or other programs related to extreme poverty and related problems in poor and predominantly black neighborhoods.

39. Chicago Public Schools, *School Funding Database* (March 2004).

40. Consortium on Chicago School Research, "Selected Indicators."

41. Gary Orfield and Chungmei Lee, "*Brown* at 50: King's Dream or *Plessy*'s Nightmare?" (Cambridge: The Harvard Civil Rights Project, January 2004), 3.

42. Orfield and Lee, 22.

43. Richard Rothstein, *Class and Schools: Using Social, Economic, and Educational Reform to Close the Black-White Achievement Gap* (Washington, DC: Economic Policy Institute, 2004), 40, 42, 43.

44. Maureen Kelleher, "Suspensions Up in CPS," *Catalyst Chicago* (December 2004), available online at www.catalyst-chicago.org/12-04main.htm.

45. Noguera, *Big City Schools*, 120–121.

46. Kelleher, "Suspensions Up."

47. Rothstein, *Class and Schools*, 46.

48. Rothstein, 19–22.

49. Christopher Jencks and Meredith Phillips, eds., *The Black-White Test-Score Gap* (Washington, DC: Brookings Institution Press, 1998), 3–9.

50. Diana White, Dennis Kass, Lee Ann Lodder, Scott McFarland and Paul Street, *Racial Preference and Suburban Employment Opportunities: A Report on "Matched-Pair" Tests of Chicago-Area Retailers* (Chicago, IL: Chicago Legal Assistance Foundation and Chicago Urban League, 2003). See also Margery Austin Turner, Michael Fix, and Raymond J. Struyk *Opportunities Denied, Opportunities Diminished: Racial Discrimination in Hiring* (Washington, DC: The Urban Institute Press, 1991).

51. Sendhill Mullainathan and Mary Ann Bertrand, "Are Emily and Brendan More Employable than Lakisha and Jamal? A Field Experiment on Labor Market Discrimination" (National Bureau of Economic Research, 2002).

52. See the excellent discussion of values, jobs, and poverty in David M. Gordon, *Fat and Mean: The Corporate Squeeze of Working Americans and the Myth of Managerial Downsizing* (New York: The Free Press, 1996), 115–139. See also Paul Street, *Vicious Circle*; Paul Street, *Still Separate, Unequal*, 130-133; Street, "Skipping Past Structural Racism."

53. Mendell and Little, "Poverty, Crime." Wilson, it is worthy noting, wrote a supportive introduction to Anyon's *Ghetto Schooling*, arguing that "the cumulative effects of economic and political decisions in the larger urban context have…severely constrained the ability and actions of current actors in city schools, including their efforts to achieve meaningful school reform. These effects are embodied in the poverty and social isolation of neighborhoods." Anyon, *Ghetto Schooling*, ix.

54. Street, "Skipping Over Structural Racism;" Paul Street, "Bill Cosby and White America," *ZNet Magazine* (May 13, 2004), available online at http://www.zmag.org/content/showarticle.cfm?ItemID=5631; Street, *Still Separate, Unequal*, 133.

55. Manning Marable, *The Great Wells of Democracy: The Meaning of Race in American Life* (New York: Basic, 2002), 15.

56. Noguera, *City Schools*, p. 144; National Resource Council, *Community Programs to Promote Youth Development* (Washington, DC: National Academy Press, 2002).

57. Giroux, *Abandoned Generation*, 74–75.

58. Irons, *Jim Crow's Children*, 345.

59. George W. Bush, comments during Presidential Debate, October 13, 2004, available online at http://www.debates.org/pages/trans20od.html.

60. Rothstein, *Class and Schools*, 130.

61. Stephanie Banchero and Darnell Little, "New Rules Help Raise Test Scores: Schools Learning How to Navigate Federal Reforms," *Chicago Tribune* (December 15, 2004), sec. 1, p. 1.

62. Rosalind Rossi, "Which Chicago Public Schools Need Rebirth?," *Chicago Sun Times*, November 18, 2004.

63. Schrag, *Final Test*, 110.

64. Rothstein, *Class and School*, 129.

65. Jencks, *Inequality*, 265.

66. Rothstein, *Class and Schools*, 130

CHAPTER 5

1. Martin Luther King, Jr., "Where Do We Go From Here?" (1967), in Washington, ed., *A Testament of Hope,* 251.

2. W.E.B. DuBois, "Postscript," *The Crisis* (January 1934), 20.

3. Douglas S. Massey, "American Apartheid: Housing Segregation and Persistent Urban Poverty," Distinguished Lecture, Social Science Research Institute (DeKalb, IL: Northern Illinois University, 1994).

4. "Expert Report of Thomas J. Sugrue" (1996), *Gratz et al. v. Bollinger,* Section VIII, available online at http://www.umich.edu/~urel/admissions/legal/expert/sugru8.html.

5. Sheryll Cashin, *The Failures of Integration: How Race and Class Are Undermining the American Dream* (New York: Public Affairs, 2004), 3–4.

6. Lawrence Bobo, "Keeping the Linchpin in Place: Testing the Multiple Sources of Opposition to Residential Integration," *Revue Internationale de Psychologie Sociale*, 2 (1980): 306–323.

7. Martin Luther King, speech at Ohio Northern University (1967), available online at http://www.onu.edu/library/onuhistory.king/king.htm.

8. Maria Krysan and Reynolds Farley, "The Residential Preference of Blacks: Do They Explain Persistent Segregation?" *Social Forces,* March 2002, 80 (3): 937–980.

9. Cashin, *The Failures of Integration,* xii–xiii.

10. Interview with an anonymous U.S. History Instructor at a leading Illinois adult correctional facility, December 18, 2003. These sentiments find empirical support in Leonard Rubinowitz and James

Rosenbaum's provocative *Crossing the Class and Color Lines: From Public Housing to White Suburbia* (Chicago: University of Chicago Press, 2000). Rosenbaum and Rubinowitz found a unique research source among the roughly 6,000 low-income African American families that were relocated from Chicago public housing to non-majority black communities during the 1980s and 1990s. The authors discovered major differences in employment and educational outcomes between families assigned to the suburbs and those assigned to other neighborhoods within the city. Those who went to the suburbs did significantly better in both areas. Leonard Rubinowitz and James Rosenbaum, *Crossing the Class and Color Lines: From Public Housing to White Suburbia* (Chicago, 2000), 161–173.

11. John Logan, *Separate and Unequal: The Neighborhood Gap for Blacks and Hispanics* (Lewis Mumford Center for Comparative Urban and Regional Research, 2002); John Logan, "The Suburban Advantage: New Census Data Show Unyielding City-Suburb Economic Gap (State University of New York at Albany: Lewis Mumford Center for Comparative Urban and Regional Research, 2002).

12. Massey, "American Apartheid."

13. Orfield and Lee, 23.

14. Noguera, *City Schools*, xi.

15. Abigail and Stephen Thernstrom, *No Excuses: Closing the Racial Gap in Learning* (New York: Simon and Schuster, 2004). Some of these program and study names are presented in a critical vein in Traub, "What No School Can Do."

16. Abigail and Stephen Thernstrom, *America in Black and White: One Nation, Indivisible* (New York: Simon and Schuster, 1999).

17. Rothstein, *Class and Schools*, 64–65.

18. Rothstein, *Class and Schools,* 71–75; Samuel Casey Carter, *No Excuses: Lessons From 21 High-Performing, High-Poverty Schools* (Washington, DC: The Heritage Foundation, 2000).

19. Rothstein, *Class and Schools*, 80–82.

20. Valerie E. Lee, *Restructuring High Schools for Equity and Excellence* (New York: Teachers College Press, 2001), 37–38, 60.

21. Diane Jean Schemo, "A Second Report Shows Charter School Students Not Performing As Well as Other Students," *New York Times* (December 16, 2004).

22. Dan French, Center for Collaborative Education, Boston MA, comments (December 14, 2004) at http://groups.yahoo.com/group/smallschools/message/4134.

23. Teresa Mendez, "Is a Smaller School Always a Better School?," *Christian Science Monitor*, December 14, 2004.

24. Giroux, *The Abandoned Generation*, 77, 78, 81, 82.

25. Thomas S. Poetter and Kathleen Knight-Abowitz, "Possibilities and Problems of School Choice," *Kappa Delta Phi Record* (Winter 2001): 58–62; Dale McDonald, "A Chronology of Parental Choice," *Momentum* (May 2001): 10–15.

26. McDonald, "A Chronology."

27. George Archibald and T. Lively, "Voucher Program Approved for D.C.," *Washington Times*, January 23, 2004.

28. Dennis Anthony Kass, "The School Voucher Debate: A Briefing Paper," Chicago Urban League, April 2002.

29. Kass, "Voucher Debate;" Terry Moe, "Cooking Questions," Education Next (Spring 2002), 71–77; David A. Bositis, 1999 National Opinion Poll, Joint Center for Political and Economic Studies; Public Agenda, "On Thin Ice: How Advocates and Opponents Could Misread the Public's Views on Vouchers and Public Schools" (2001), poll at http://www.publicagenda.org/specialis/vouchers/ voucherfinding1. htm.

30. Daniel P. Mayer et al., *School Choice in New York City After Three Years* (Mathematica Policy Research, Inc, 2002).

31. Kass; John F. Witte, "Achievement Effects of the Milwaukee Voucher Program," paper presented at the 1997 American Economic Association's Annual Meetings; Cecilia Rouse; Jay P. Green, "The Surprising Consensus on School Choice," *The Public Interest* (Summer 2001); May Ann Zeher, "Effects of Vouchers on Achievement Unclear," Education Week (November 11, 2001); General Accounting Office, "School Vouchers: Publicly Funded Programs in Cleveland and Milwaukee" (Washington, DC: GAO, August 2001).

32. Kim K. Metcalf and Polly Tait, "Free Market Policies and Public Education: What is the Cost of Choice?," *Phi Delta Kappan* (September 1999): 65–75.

33. National Education Association, "School Vouchers: The Emerging Track Record" (April 2002), available online at www.nea.org/issues/ vouchers/02voutrack.html.

34. Gerald Bracey, "The Eleventh Bracey Report on the Condition of Public Education," *Phi Delta Kappan* (October 1999): 147–168.

35. Rethinking Schools, *False Choices: Vouchers, Public Schools, and Our Children's Future* (2002), available online at http://www.rethinking-schools.org/SpecPub/vouchers/vcollect.htm.

36. Paul Street and Dennis Kass, "The Case Against School Vouchers," *Z Magazine* (July 2002), available online at http://www.zmag.org/content/print_article.cfm?itemID=2054&sectionID=30; Cashin, *Failures of Integration*, 300.

37. John Margolis, "Voters and Vouchers," *American Prospect* (May 2001): 22–23.

38. Public Agenda, "On Thin Ice;" David Bositis, *1999 National Opinion Poll.*

39. Kass, "Voucher Debate;" Moe, "Cooking Questions;" Jennifer Hochschild and Bridgett Scott, "Trends: Governance and Reform of Public Education in the United States," *Public Opinion Quarterly*, 62 (1998): 79–120.

40. Cashin, *The Failures of Integration*, 300; Street and Kass, "The Case Against Vouchers."

41. Supreme Court Justice David Souter, Dissenting opinion in *Zell v. Simmons-Harris* (June 27, 2002), available online at http://caselaw.lp.findlaw.com/scripts/getcase.pl?court=US&vol=000&invol=00-1751#section5l; Rethinking Schools, "Supreme Court Debates Vouchers" (2002), available online at www.rethinkingschools.org/SpecPub/vouchers/vdeba.htm. Revealingly enough, given its clear connection to religious and especially Christian schools circles, the voucher movement sends a spiritually troubling message regarding the disproportionately minority children of the urban poor. At best, voucher schemes permit a relatively small number of the better-scoring and more well off inner-city students with the most educated parents to attend private schools, leaving the most disadvantaged behind in the supposedly failing public schools. It is more ethically consistent and egalitarian, however, to work to save those public schools by addressing the full array of educational and societal inequalities that create enormous difficulties in the nation's hyper-segregated inner-city schools.

42. Amy Gutman, "What Does 'School Choice' Mean?," *Dissent* (Summer 2000), 23.

43. Noguera, *City Schools*, 82–102.

44. Rothstein, *Class and Schools*, 61–83.

45. Among many possible sources and reflections, see Cashin, *The Failures of Integration*; Steinhorn and Diggs-Brown, *By the Color of Our Skin*; Street, *Still Separate, Unequal*; Massey, "American Apartheid."

46. National Priorities Project, "Costs of Iraq War" (2004), available online at http://database.nationalpriorities.org.

47. National Priorities Project, "Education Finding Falls Short" (2004), available online at http://www.nationalpriorities.org/issues/edu/fallingshort/index.html.

48. National Priorities Project, "Where Do Your Tax Dollars Go?" (April 2004), available online at http://www.nationalpriorities.org/Tax-Day/2004/pdf/us.pdf.

49. Issac Shapiro and Joe Friedman. "Tax Returns: A Comprehensive Assessment of the Bush Administration's Record on Cutting Taxes" (Washington, DC: Center for Budget and Policy Priorities, April 23, 2004).

50. American Federation of Teachers, *2003 Survey and Analysis of Teacher Salary Trends,* available online at http://www.aft.org/salary/.

51. Jacki Calmes, "Sharpening the Knife: Bush Vows to Halve Deficit, Targets Already Feel Squeezed," *Wall Street Journal,* December 21, 2001, A1).

52. Justice Policy Institute, *Cell Blocks or Classrooms?* (Washington, DC Justice Policy Institute, August 2002); Street, *The Vicious Circle.*

53. Paul Street, *Empire and Inequality: America and the World Since 9/11* (Boulder, CO: Paradigm Publishers, 2004), xiii–xiv, 143–171; Pierre Bordieu, *Acts of Resistance* (New York: Free Press, 1998), 2, 24–44; Noam Chomsky, *Chomsky on Democracy and Education,* edited by C. P. Otero (New York: RoutledgeFalmer, 2003), 36–37; Chomsky, *Profits Over People,* 65–120; John Pilger, *The New Rulers of the World* (London: Verso, 2002), 5, 116; Boris Kargalitsky, "Facing the Crisis," *Links,* No. 1 (September-December 2001); Giroux, *The Abandoned Generation,* xiii–102; Paul Street and Henry A. Giroux, "Shredding the Social Contract," *ZNet Magazine* (September 4, 2003), available online at http://www.zmag.org/content/showarticle.cfm?ItemID=4133&SectionID=11; Paul Street, "Mass Incarceration and Racist State Priorities At Home and Abroad," *ZNet Magazine* (March 4, 2003), at http://www.zmag.org and http://www.minorityx.com/viewarticle.php?artId=140; Paul Street, "Starve the Racist Prison Beast," *Black Commentator,* Issue 65 (November 20, 2003), available online at http://www.blackcommentator.com.

54. Street, *Empire and Inequality,* xvi.

55. David Nibert, *Hitting the Lottery Jackpot: Government and the Taxing of Dreams* (New York: Monthly Review Press, 2000), 87–105; Giroux, *The Abandoned Generation,* 38. See also Charles Clotfelter and Phillip Cook, *Selling Hope: State Lotteries in America* (Cambridge: Harvard University Press, 1989).

56. Paul Street, "More Than Entertainment: Neal Gabler and the Illusions of Post-Ideological Society," *Monthly Review* (February 2000): 58–62; Paul Street, "Thought Control," *ZNet Magazine* (April 27, 2004), available online at http://www.zmag.org/content/showarticle.cfm?SectionID=21&ItemID=5410; Paul Street, "Killing Us Softly: Politics and Entertainment," *ZNet Magazine* (April 21, 2004), available online at http://www.zmag.org/content/showarticle.cfm?SectionID=21&ItemID=5372. According to Giroux, "educators must challenge the assumption that education is limited to schooling and that popular culture texts cannot be as profoundly important as traditional sources of learning in teaching about important issues, for example, poverty, racial conflict, and gender discrimination." Giroux, op cit, 38.

57. In his book *Final Test*, school funding adequacy advocate Peter Schrag is reluctant to address the toxic and authoritarian impact of America's standardized-testing on poor and minority children in segregated schools. He prefers to use the testing industry—more specifically that industry's test-measured achievement gap—as a weapon in the struggle for school funding adequacy. It is interesting to note, however, that the Latino and black high school students who joined the ACLU school funding lawsuit that was favorably highlighted in Schrag's book were motivated to fight against California's school funding inequalities after reading (by Schrag's account) a selection from radical pedagogy theorist Paulo Freire's *Pedagogy of the Oppressed,* which was assigned to them by a politically engaged social studies teacher. See Schrag, *Final Test,* 18. Freire would certainly have recognized the current American skill and drill test-based curriculum as a variation on what he denounced in 1960s Brazil as "the banking concept of education."

58. Chomsky, *On Democracy and Education,* 25–42; Noam Chomsky, *World Orders Old and New* (New York: Columbia University Press, 1994, 1996), 87.

Index